Duelling Through
the Ages

Duelling Through the Ages

Stephen Wynn

Pen & Sword
MILITARY
AN IMPRINT OF PEN & SWORD BOOKS LTD.
YORKSHIRE - PHILADELPHIA

First published in Great Britain in 2021 by
Pen & Sword Military
An imprint of
Pen & Sword Books Ltd
Yorkshire - Philadelphia

ISBN 978 1 52673 853 0

Printed and bound in England
By CPI Group (UK) Ltd, Croydon, CR0 4YY

Pen & Sword Books Ltd. incorporates the Imprints of Pen & Sword
Archaeology, Atlas, Aviation, Battleground, Discovery, Family History,
History, Maritime, Military, Naval, Politics, Railways, Select, Transport,
True Crime, Fiction, Frontline Books, Leo Cooper, Praetorian Press,
Seaforth Publishing, Wharncliffe and White Owl.

For a complete list of Pen & Sword titles please contact

PEN & SWORD BOOKS LIMITED
47 Church Street, Barnsley, South Yorkshire, S70 2AS, England
E-mail: enquiries@pen-and-sword.co.uk
Website: www.pen-and-sword.co.uk

or

PEN AND SWORD BOOKS
1950 Lawrence Rd, Havertown, PA 19083, USA
E-mail: uspen-and-sword@casematepublishers.com
Website: www.penandswordbooks.com

MIX
Paper from
responsible sources
FSC
www.fsc.org   FSC® C013604

This book is dedicated to all front-line staff, no matter what role they performed in keeping their communities safe and the country running, and also in memory of the tens of thousands of people who sadly died during the Covid-19 virus pandemic throughout the course of 2020–21.

Contents

Introduction

❖

One description of the word duel, albeit a nineteenth century one, is:

> *'A pre-arranged combat between two persons, fought with deadly weapons according to an accepted code of procedure, especially, but not specifically, to settle a private disagreement.'*

As such events were, more often than not, the sole domain of officers and gentlemen, the rules by which they were undertaken were based on the medieval code of chivalry, and concerned a man's reputation and honour, which for some men are still of importance even today. It was a way in which men could resolve a disagreement between themselves if they felt that they had been wronged by another, usually verbally, but not exclusively so.

For some, a duel also provided them with the ability to quarrel with somebody (who might not be as capable as themselves), with the sole intention of acquiring their wealth and belongings.

To achieve this was a simple process. Identify a wealthy individual, call him a coward, accuse him of being a liar, or claim the individual had slurred the accuser in some made up words or deeds. In such a case, if the wealthy individual didn't challenge his accuser to a duel, his own reputation would be at stake, as it would be assumed that by not doing so it meant the initial accusation or slur must be true.

A more difficult scenario I struggle to contemplate, was the one of 'turning the other cheek' i.e. ignoring the perceived or intended slur on one's character and simply walking away. The 'injured' party would demand satisfaction from their accuser in what today might be seen as the somewhat theatrical manner of throwing a glove on the ground in front of them. At the time, such a gesture was viewed as being extremely insulting, leaving the recipient of the act with only one real course of action: to pick up the glove, and accept the challenge.

In essence, a man was damned if he did and damned if he didn't. Looking back on it now, it all seems so very childish and little more than a petulant infant demanding to get its own way, and resorting to throwing a tantrum, or a fit of pique, when it didn't. But at the time, a man's reputation, especially in the ranks of the nobility and the upper classes, was everything.

Now we know why duels took place, the next point to clarify is the process. By this I mean the choice of weapons, which understandably had to be exactly the same for both men. You obviously couldn't have a scenario when one man had a doubled-handed long sword whilst the other had a foil. Most duels during the late sixteenth, seventeenth and eighteenth centuries were fought with swords, usually rapiers, but by the late eighteenth century, many duels in England were conducted using pistols.

Duelling can be traced back to the medieval period of history as well as the time of the Roman Empire. In 1215, legislation against it as an activity was brought in by the Fourth Council of the Lateran, which in laymen's terms, means a council that was convoked by Pope Innocent III, at Rome's Lateran Palace, beginning on 11 November 1215.

In the immediate wake of the Thirty Years War, which was fought predominantly throughout Central Europe between 1618 and 1648, in what was known at the time as the Holy Roman Empire, civil legislation was passed to prevent duelling from taking place.

Through the pages of this book I will explore what duelling looked like during the different periods and countries it took place in. I will also look at the rules and regulations which governed duelling, its decline and outlawing, and its eventual inclusion in the Olympic Games.

CHAPTER ONE

General Overview

❖

A duel fought between members of the aristocracy, military personnel and gentlemen during the seventeenth, eighteenth and nineteenth centuries throughout most of western Europe, was a different affair to say that of a fight between gladiators in Roman times, samurai warriors engaging in Ikki-uchi, or gunfights in the American Wild West, where the overall intention was for a man to defeat and/or kill his opponent. But in their own way, each of these different variations was a duel, with one man pitting his wits and fighting skills against an adversary with the aim of beating him.

The European version of duelling was also practised in America throughout the seventeenth and eighteenth centuries, but only between the very elite of society, where it was viewed more as a matter of honour and respect; important issues for most men of the day.

So as not to cause confusion whilst examining the different versions of duelling, for clarity I will separate the British, Roman and European versions. Many of the earlier versions of the practice were conducted solely with the use of a sword or rapier, but by the end of the late eighteenth and turn of the early nineteenth century, most duels were carried out with pistols, although not exclusively. Duelling (as in the

European version), had all but ceased throughout America by the end of the American Civil War in 1865.

In medieval times, judicial duels, i.e. those that were officially acknowledged and approved by a king or his parliament, were commonplace in society throughout Britain, Ireland and most of Europe. Such duels were nearly always to do with a personal slight to somebody's honour, which hadn't been resolved through that country's court system.

Although the word honour was used hand in hand with the word duel, there was very little honour in the way a man dealt with his defeated enemy. The weapons used, such as longswords, axes, polearms – which would more readily be recognised as a pike or lance – and the misericordia, a long, narrow knife that was specifically used to deliver the death stroke to a knight in battle, had no other purpose other than to kill.

There was no time limit for these duels, it was simply a case of fighting until one party could continue no longer. If the vanquished man wasn't killed, he could be executed, no matter how gallantly he had fought. More often than not, judicial duels included the caveat of having to be fought to the death.

In the late fourteenth and throughout the fifteenth century, and originating out of events such as judicial duels, things got slightly out of hand when knights who wanted to prove themselves became involved in what was known as the 'passage of arms'. This involved being aware of routes commonly used by travellers that came to a pinch point – such as a bridge or a city gate – specific locations that people had to pass to be able to continue their journey. Such knights would make it known that if any other knights wished to pass, they would first have to fight, knowing that if the challenge was turned down, then the passing knight would be shamed and forced to leave his spurs behind to confirm his humiliation.

Religion and God played a large part in medieval times, and the Catholic Church was vehemently against any kind of duelling, where killing one's opponent was the main purpose of the contest, but the practice of judicial duelling persisted as late as the time of the Holy Roman Empire; well into the fifteenth century.

It didn't really matter what word one chose to use to describe two men fighting each other, it amounted to the same thing. This becomes even clearer when looking at the word 'duel', which was used almost to sanitise the brutal and barbaric act of two men fighting each other with either swords or pistols, to make it sound more gentlemanly and about honour. The origins of the word 'duel' are born out of the Latin word *duellum* which was cognate with the word *bellum*, meaning war.

The Renaissance period of European history, which covered the fifteenth and sixteenth centuries, saw an acceptability and respectability of duelling, despite earlier attempts by the Church, kings and parliaments to bring an end to its practice throughout the Middle Ages. Duelling became the sole domain of the aristocracy, officers in the military, and gentlemen in civilian life, who saw it as a way to resolve disputes between themselves, especially if it was to do with a personal slight or a matter of honour, perceived or otherwise. There were those who even saw it as a badge of honour, believing that to have been involved in, and survived, a duel gave them some kind of manly kudos over their contemporaries.

In 1626, King Louis XIII of France went as far as making the practice of duelling an offence. After his death, his successor Louis XIV continued with the same approach and even intensified the efforts of finally bringing duelling to an end, once and for all. Between 1685 and 1716, some ninety years after it had been outlawed, an estimated 400 French officers had been killed as a result of having taken part in a duel.

Between 1798 and the beginning of the American Civil War in 1861, the United States navy lost two-thirds as many officers to duelling as they did in combat at sea.

The first code of duelling was published in Italy in 1409, by Fiore dei Liberi, who was a knight, a diplomat and a fencing master. A copy of his illustrated manuscript entitled *Fior di Battaglia*, or The Flower of Battle, still exists and is held at the Morgan Library and Museum in New York.

The purpose of this code was to regulate duelling and in doing so, help prevent matters escalating out of control in the aftermath of a duel, where families of the losers might consider seeking revenge for their loss. The code also covered issues such as medical care, seconds and witnesses, and even the prevention of the duel from actually taking place. The seconds of participants would try and reconcile the differences between the two men involved by attempting to settle the dispute with an apology or some kind of acceptable restitution. If these attempts were successful, everybody was happy, the participants' honour was still intact, and both men returned to their home and families without a shot being fired.

By as early as 1770 in England, the weapon of choice to be used in a duel changed from being a sword to a pistol. It was a change that was greeted reasonably enthusiastically by those who were inclined to engage in the practice. The use of a sword up until that point in history was in keeping with the dress code of the day, where it was common practice for the wearing of a sword as a part of a man's everyday attire. But as fashions changed over the years and the wearing of swords became less fashionable after the turn of the nineteenth century, pistols not only replaced swords in society but in duels as well, although duelling with swords did continue until duelling was no more.

Duelling with swords was usually conducted in a marked-out square, with the corners identified with handkerchiefs. To begin with, the participants would stand some twenty paces apart, and if either man left the confines of the marked-out square, he was considered a coward. Having a reputation as a coward not only affected a man's reputation and social standing in society, but that of his immediate family also. It wasn't a word that anybody wanted to be called.

The most common way for a duel to come to a conclusion was when one party was physically unable to continue, or the doctor who was in attendance called a halt to the proceedings. What were known as 'first blood' duels weren't encouraged as they were seen as being unmanly and dishonourable, as all one party had to do was to draw blood, which could be achieved by a slight scratch on a man's arm or face. The system was open to abuse; participants could pre-plan a duel, where one of the pair would draw blood, thereby ending the duel. Honour was sated and both men returned home.

By the late eighteenth century, the world had changed greatly. It was now what history has recorded as the 'Enlightenment Era', where politeness and civility became the driving forces throughout British and European society. Power-crazed kings and armour-wearing knights had been replaced by intellectuals and philosophers and the thirst for violence had at long last been quenched. In the brave new world of the Enlightenment, there was no room for or acceptance of the violent behaviour that had become a byword and relic of England's and Europe's medieval past.

For me, there were really interesting aspects of this new era. One was what today would be known as policing. From the Middle Ages there had been village and town constables, whose job it was to keep the peace. It was an unpaid position which was held for a year at a time. The constable, on being informed that a crime had been committed, raised the alarm, which galvanised the local men to catch the man responsible. This was known as raising the 'hue and cry'. It was obviously a successful system as it stayed in place until 1827.

Paid night watchmen appeared from 1663 and were employed to guard and protect mainly industrial premises from the clutches of wanton burglars. It was a dangerous job as the watchmen tended to be old and the burglars could be extremely violent if the need arose. Over 100 years later, many local town authorities began paying night watchmen to patrol the streets during the hours of darkness to help keep their communities safe from unwanted interlopers.

The biggest breakthrough without a doubt took place in 1749 with the formation of the Bow Street Runners by a London Magistrate named Henry Fielding. They weren't a police service as such, instead they went looking for criminals, with warrants issued for their arrest by the magistrates' courts.

In 1798, with London's shipping making the capital the nation's busiest port, the River Police was formed to help protect the ships' cargoes from the clutches of the city's evil and violent gangs.

All of the above interventions finally came to a head in 1829 with the creation of the Metropolitan Police by Sir Robert Peel, with the new constables being affectionately referred to as 'Bobbies' or 'Peelers'.

The other aspect I want to take a brief look at, which remains an extremely important one, was the move away from the gun or sword for recompense by men who felt they had been slighted, disrespected or that they had their honour called into question. No longer were they so quick to challenge another to a duel. One of the reasons behind this was the emergence of newspapers. The burgeoning number of the middle classes of society instead sought to bring charges of libel against their accuser before the courts, or by way of correspondence in one of the ever-increasing volume of daily and weekly newspapers that had begun to appear throughout the eighteenth century. It was in keeping with the more civilised approach and attitudes to the civility and politeness of everyday life.

In 1838, American John Lyde Wilson (1784–1849) published what he entitled 'The Code of Honor', a set of rules for the government, principals and seconds in duelling. It began with an address to the public followed by eight chapters. It is too long and detailed a document to include within the pages of this book, but can be summarised briefly as follows:

Chapter 1. The Person insulted, before the challenge sent (7 separate points).

Chapter 2. Second's duty before challenge sent (10 separate points).

Chapter 3. The Party receiving a note before Challenge (6 separate points).

Chapter 4. Duty of challenge and second after challenge sent (2 separate points).

Chapter 5. Duty of principals and seconds on the ground (10 separate points).

Chapter 6. Who should be on the ground (3 separate points).

Chapter 7. Arms and manner of presenting them (4 separate points).

Chapter 8. The degrees of insult and how comprised (7 separate points).

A second edition, published in 1858, included an appendix which somewhat strangely began with the following.

'Since the above code was in press, a friend has favoured me with the IRISH CODE OF HONOR, which I had never seen, and it is published as an appendix to it.'

It then listed the twenty-five rules of the Irish duelling code of 1777.

An interesting intervention came into being in 1867, when John Graham Chambers wrote what he entitled the 'Marquess of Queensberry Rules', for the ever popular practice of pugilism: fisticuffs undertaken by gentlemen. This really was a classic case of 'necessity being the mother of all invention'. The Irish Code issued in relation to duelling had been seen by many people as far too dangerous, without that being an odd thing to say. For many, duelling was simply a means to end, with most people having no intention or desire to kill the person they were fighting, all they wanted was the ability to either save or redeem their honour.

The decline in duelling hastened after the 1840 case of the 7th Earl of Cardigan, who killed one of his former officers after fighting with him in a duel. The earl was tried for manslaughter and acquitted on a legal technicality. The decision caused public outrage, which was fuelled by elements of the press. This included *The Times*, which alleged that there was complicity at the highest level to ensure the earl wasn't found guilty and that 'in England there is one law for the rich and another for the poor', whilst *The Examiner* led with the title, 'A defeat of justice'.

Cardigan was tried in 1841, not before a criminal court, but before the House of Lords, which as a nobleman was his right in law at the time. This meant that those listening to the evidence of the case were the other 120 members of the House of Lords. The charge against him was that he had fired upon Captain Harvey Tuckett, but as it was proved that the man's name was actually Harvey Garnet Phipps Tuckett, this was deemed to have been of sufficient discrepancy to allow his 120 peers to acquit him of the charge.

By 1841, even though the practice of duelling had declined massively, it was still going on, possibly because there was a two-handed approach to the problem. This had come about because duelling was the sole domain of the aristocracy and gentlemen. A good example of this was the United Kingdom, where to kill someone in a duel was formally deemed to be a case of murder, but rarely did the courts prosecute such affairs – mainly because they were sympathetic towards a man fighting another man over the issue of honour. In the case of the 7th Earl of Cardigan, even Queen Victoria was said to have expressed the opinion that she hoped that he 'would get off easily'. Would she have made the same comment if the person in question had been of a lesser standing in society or somebody who was unknown to her? We can never know.

The other aspect of this duel was more to do with the manner in which Cardigan conducted himself. He had used what was described as a 'sophisticated' duelling pistol, which had concealed rifling and a hair trigger – thought to be somewhat unsportsmanlike according to the 'rules' of duelling. Maybe it was his notoriety as the man who led the charge of the Light Brigade during the Crimean War. Of the 674 men who took part in the famous charge, 107 were killed, with an additional unknown number of those who died of their wounds. Cardigan had expressed his doubts about the attack, but went ahead with it only after he was given a direct order to do so by his superior officer, Lord Lucan, who had conveyed his message via Captain Louis Nolan, who was one of those killed in the attack. With Nolan dead, both men chose to blame him by having incorrectly relayed the message, not because they knew that to be a fact, but possibly in an effort to save their own reputations.

By the 1850s, duelling with either pistol or sword was all but a thing of the past. Although it still went on, it no longer had the same appeal that it once had and many countries had made the practice illegal, with the consequences for being engaged in a duel extremely severe and many exponents of the practice being tried for manslaughter and murder.

In America it appears to have taken the bloodshed and slaughter of the Civil War (1861-65), which resulted in more than 618,000 deaths, or 600 people every single day, to change attitudes towards duelling.

In the first half of the nineteenth century, in the South and throughout the Western Frontier where law enforcement was maybe not quite as strong and as visible as it needed to be, duelling was generally still viewed in a positive light. This was after the attempts during the latter part of the eighteenth century by both Benjamin Franklin, one of the nation's Founding Fathers, and George Washington, a Founding Father, President and leader of the victorious and patriotic forces in the War of Independence, to bring an end to the practice.

The problem was that honour, respect, credibility and social standing still played an extremely important part in society, especially if a man was in the military, a gentleman or a member of the aristocracy. If men weren't going to become involved in duelling, then they most definitely needed something to replace it.

Pugilism had been particularly popular in Venice since the twelfth century, and had made its way to England in around 1615, when a London arms master had begun offering lessons in its required skills to the gentry. Gradually it grew in popularity.

In the years that followed, many men attempted, and failed, to come up with a suitable and acceptable set of rules to govern the art of pugilism that the majority could agree on as a way forward.

John Graham Chambers was a Welshman and a keen sportsman. But the word that best describes him is phenomenon. Whilst at Cambridge University he was a member of the rowing team that lost to Oxford in both 1862 and 1863, as well as coaching them to four victories against Oxford between 1871 and 1874, in what is today known as the 'boat race'. He was a driving force in the organisation of inter-university sports, a champion walker, and helped arrange and stage the FA Cup final as well as the prestigious Thames Regatta annual boating gala. He rowed alongside Matthew Webb as he swam the English Channel in 1875 from Dover to Calais in under twenty-two hours. He was also responsible for beginning and organising national championships in athletics, billiards, boxing, cycling, and wrestling.

When Chambers created his set of rules for those keen to become involved in pugilism, rather than call them 'Chambers' Rules', he came up with the idea of having them supported by a member of society with an impeccable social standing to give his rules some credence and impact. He turned to John Sholto

Douglas, 9th Marquess of Queensberry, who agreed to endorse them. Chambers and the Marquess were both Cambridge men, having studied at the university at the same time.

The 9th Marquess of Queensberry was a character in his own right. Prior to entering Magdalene College at Cambridge University in 1864, he had served as an officer in the Royal Navy and between 1869 and 1871, was a lieutenant colonel in charge of the 1st Dumfriesshire Rifle Volunteers. His third son, Lord Alfred 'Bosie' Douglas, was rumoured to have been the lover of the famous author and poet Oscar Wilde.

The marquess was a noted sporting enthusiast, with boxing being his main interest. In 1866 he founded the Amateur Athletic Club, known today as the Amateur Athletic Association of England. Before the marquess founded his club, amateur athletes had to belong to the upper classes to be able to compete.

It was the following year that the Amateur Athletic Club published Chambers' twelve rules for boxing, under the marquess's sponsorship. The twelve rules were as follows:

1. To be a fair stand-up boxing match in a 24-ft ring, or as near that size as practicable.
2. No wrestling allowed.
3. The rounds to be of three minutes' duration, and one minute's time between rounds.
4. If either man falls through weakness or otherwise, he must get up unassisted, ten seconds to be allowed him to do so, the other man meanwhile to return to his corner, and when the fallen man is on his legs the round is to be resumed and continued until the three minutes have expired. If one man fails to come to the scratch in the ten seconds allowed, it shall be in the power of the referee to give his award in favour of the other man.

5. A man hanging on the ropes in a helpless state, with his toes off the ground, shall be considered down.

6. No seconds or any other person to be allowed in the ring during the rounds.

7. Should the contest be stopped by an unavoidable interference, the referee to name the time and place as soon as possible for finishing the contest; so that the match must be won and lost, unless the backers of both men agree to draw the stakes.

8. The gloves to be fair-sized boxing gloves of the best quality and new.

9. Should a glove burst, or come off, it must be replaced to the referee's satisfaction.

10. A man on one knee is considered down and if struck entitled to the stakes.

11. That no shoes or boots with spikes or sprigs [wire nails] be allowed.

12. The contest in all other respects to be governed by revised London Prize Ring Rules.

In essence, although they have been improved on with three judges determining the winner, the inclusion of a technical knockout, a standing eight count, no hitting below the belt, no kicking, head-butting, striking with any part of the arm other than their fists, much of the original rules are still part of what makes boxing what it is today.

Chambers' rules were a far less dangerous method than resorting to the use of a gun or a sword for two gentlemen to decide their differences. Two men could fight with their fists; there would be a winner and a loser, but both men's honour and pride would still be intact at the end of it.

And so it was that the art of pugilism slowly but surely replaced the practice of duelling. Men, at long last realised that to right a wrong, and to protect their honour, they no longer had to risk losing their life and their family's livelihood and wellbeing by fighting a man with a sword or a pistol. It had only taken the intervention of John Graham Chambers, with his Queensberry Rules, and more than 1,000 years, to actually work it out.

When it came to rules, Europe wasn't the only place where they differed according to where in the country a man lived. America had a Southern United States duelling code of honour and a Western United States code of honour.

Duels in the South continued throughout the 1840s, even though by that time duelling was illegal throughout the entire country. It was made even more complicated by the fact that many of the Southern states had their own rules for duelling. When such events did take place, it was very rare that the protagonists were prosecuted, possibly because those who took part were nearly always from the upper classes of society.

I have written in depth elsewhere in the book about the Wild Bill Hickok gunfight in July of 1865, which is one of the first known quick-fire duels that took place in America's Wild West. An equally interesting and notable duel took place on 19 August 1871, at Hide Park in Newton, Kansas, between Hugh Anderson and Mike McCluskey. What gave this duel a certain amount of notoriety was it was fought with both pistols and knifes.

Although reported at the time and having a higher body count than the one at the OK Corral, the gunfight at Hide Park has not remained at the forefront of history. This is possibly because none of those who took part were particularly well known or notable gunmen or lawmen, and none went on to become famous as a result of the confrontation.

How did it come to be? The incident began as a result of an argument between two local lawmen, Mike McCluskey and Billy Bailey, which had started on 11 August 1871 in the 'Red Front Saloon' and, maybe somewhat surprisingly for two lawmen, was over local politics. The verbal argument became so heated that it degenerated into a fight; Bailey was shoved out of the saloon and into the street, quickly followed by McCluskey, who drew his pistol and fired two shots at Bailey, who was still on the ground. One of the shots, which hit him in the chest, killed him. McCluskey didn't hang around to see what was going to happen, and fearing he would be arrested, fled town. After only a few days, he returned having heard that the matter was likely to be treated as self-defence, despite the fact that Bailey hadn't even drawn his gun. Maybe with the self-defence aspect playing on his mind, he later claimed that he feared for his life knowing that Bailey had killed two men in three previous gunfights.

On the fateful day, 19 August 1871, McCluskey was in Newton and went to the Tuttles Dance Hall with a friend of his, Jim Martin, for a drink and to play cards. This in itself was quite brave, or stupid, depending on how one looked at these matters, as several cowboy friends of Bailey were still in town and had vowed to kill McCluskey for the killing of Billy Bailey. After McCluskey and Martin had seated themselves at a table and begun playing cards, three cowboys, Billy Garrett, Henry Kearnes and Jim Wilkerson, all friends of Billy Bailey, walked into the dance hall. Shortly afterwards a man by the name of Hugh Anderson, a cowboy, known gunfighter and the son of a wealthy Texas cattle rancher, walked in and approached McCluskey, calling him a coward and threatening to kill him.

The two men became involved in a heated argument, before Jim Martin stood up to try to prevent a fight from breaking out, but he failed miserably, as Anderson drew his pistol and shot McCluskey in the neck and body, the force of the bullet knocking him to the floor. He tried to return fire but his pistol jammed. Anderson then stood over him and shot him a number of times in the back.

Even though McCluskey by this time was already dead, the three cowboys, Kearns, Garrett and Wilkerson also began shooting at him. As if the events hadn't been unusual enough, a young man made sure that the gunfight at Hide Park became one of the more famous gunfights of the old Wild West. James Riley, an 18-year-old who had been taken in by McCluskey and looked after, was in the bar at the time. As he was dying of tuberculosis, he perhaps thought he had nothing to lose, he certainly didn't seem at all concerned for his own well-being. Single-handedly he took on the four cowboys and began firing. He managed to kill Garrett and Kearns as well as wounding Anderson and Wilkerson, who both survived. Riley also managed to shoot and kill an innocent bystander by the name of Patrick Lee. He shot Jim Martin, who died the following day, in the neck. He also shot and wounded another bystander who just happened to be standing close to Anderson and Wilkerson when they were shot.

After he had finished shooting, and with his guns empty and his adversaries either dead or wounded on the dance hall floor, Riley holstered his pistol, brushed himself down, and calmly walked out of the saloon, never to be seen again.

A warrant was subsequently issued for Anderson's arrest, but he had left town and arrived in Texas before it could be actioned. After recovering from his wounds he became a bartender at a saloon in the town of Medicine Lodge in Kansas.

But that wasn't to be the end of the matter. There are two versions of what happened next, the first of which follows below.

Nearly two years later in July 1873, Mike McCluskey's brother, Arthur, who had been looking for Anderson for some considerable time, finally found him in the newly established town of Medicine Lodge, so named because of the nearby Medicine Lodge River, and challenged him to a duel. Anderson accepted the challenge and chose pistols over knives as his preferred weapon. But this really was an old-fashioned duel, it wasn't a gunfight where each man stood at opposite ends of the street and both drew their guns from the holster and fired and fast as they could.

The duel took place in the cooling heat of the late afternoon, with large numbers of townsfolk having turned up to watch. They weren't standing facing each other as might be expected of gunfights in the Wild West, but rather back-to-back with a distance of twenty paces separating them. On the sound of a gunshot, the two men turned to face each other, aimed, fired and missed. They continued firing at each other, and this time they were more successful. Two of Anderson's shots hit McCluskey in the mouth and neck, whilst in return Anderson was hit in the arm. Despite the wounds, both men were still standing. McCluskey fired again, striking Anderson in the stomach, but it was McCluskey who was the first to fall. With his remaining two shots Anderson struck McCluskey twice, but neither shot proved fatal. Rather than end the matter there, both men drew knifes and went at each other again, stabbing one another repeatedly, resulting in McCluskey falling for a second time. As he was unable to defend himself, the duel was over. McCluskey was taken to a nearby boarding house where he died of his wounds the following day. As for Anderson, what happened to him isn't so clear. Some reports say that he also died of his wounds a short time later. However, the 1880 Federal Census does record a Hugh Anderson, living with his son, Oscar, in McCulloch, Texas, where he worked as a stock raiser. He is also mentioned in the US Census for 1900. It appears that he died on 9 June 1914, at Tinnie, Lincoln County, when he was struck by lightning after having taken shelter under a tree during a storm.

CHAPTER TWO

Roman Gladiators

❖

During the Battle of Fidenae in 437 BC, between the Roman Republic and the combined forces of Fidenae and Veii, an act of single combat took place between the wealthy Etruscan King Lars Tolumnius, of Veii, a city some 10 miles north-west of Rome, and Aulus Cornelius Cossus, a Roman general and politician.

According to the Roman historian Livy, Cossus managed to unseat King Tolumnius from his trusty steed and after a fight between the two men, which lasted no longer than a matter of seconds, Cossus killed Tolumnius with his sword. Any chivalry ended there, because what happened after, even though it may well have been in keeping with the time, wouldn't have been classed as having been a respectful act by today's standards. After removing Tolumnius's armour, Cossus decapitated him and, impaling the head on the end of a lance, paraded it in front of the enemy troops, who were so shocked by the scale of the brutality of their leader's death, they hastily retreated in horror.

For his actions that day, Cossus, was given the rare award of *Spolia Opima* for killing an enemy leader in single combat. Such an award allowed the recipient to retain the armour, sword and shield, and was seen as the most honourable of the different kinds of military awards an army commander could receive.

After the battle, which was a resounding victory for the Romans, Cossus, who had brought Tolumnius's armour, sword and shield back with him to Rome, donated the items to the Temple of Jupiter Feretrius, situated on the Capitoline Hill between the Forum and the Campus Martius.

There are numerous accounts of similar feats of combat having taken place during Roman times, and although many sound extremely brave deeds, I raise two points against them. Firstly, they read more like fights than duels. The men involved had no personal gripe against each other. It was one army taking up arms against another and during that battle there would be occasions where men found themselves in single combat with members of the opposing army. These men were simply trying to kill each other. The second consideration to keep in mind with these accounts were that they were recorded by historians who, in most cases, weren't present at the events they wrote about, and who were only going to write positive accounts through fear of annoying those they were writing about – which could ultimately result in their own deaths.

I will also add that in Roman times, life was cheap, not for those who lost their lives, but for those who deemed who would live and who would die. To those in power, the life of a commoner appeared to have little in the way of value.

Whilst looking at what possibly passed as duelling during Roman times, it would be remiss of me not to include a piece on gladiators. Gladiator is a Latin word, meaning 'swordsman'. It was a job, of sorts.

Although the actual origins of gladiatorial fights are open to debate, the men who filled the roles were armed combatants whose job it was to entertain audiences at such places as the

Colosseum in ancient Rome. These events were often referred to as 'the Games', but the sports and contests involved fighting against other gladiators, wild animals and convicted criminals.

Many men fought as a particular type of gladiator, such as a *secutor*, one who fought with a sword, helmet and a chainmail sleeve, usually worn on the right arm. Then there was a *retiarius* who wore no helmet or headgear of any kind. He was only lightly armoured on his left arm and shoulder, and was armed with a trident, dagger and net. Other gladiators favoured fighting from chariots, or even horseback. There were the *damnati* or slaves, sometimes purchased by wealthy owners, who had been condemned to the arena, gladiator school, or straight into a games. This was usually as a punishment for crimes they had committed. For these men life was harsh. They were constantly under stress, a combination of the long hard hours of training, their harsh living conditions, and the ever-present threat and fear of death.

There were others, free men, who volunteered to be gladiators, but who were paid for their effort. They fought for fame and fortune and were known as *autocrati*, and by the time of the late Roman Republic made up about half of all gladiators who fought in the arenas. For some Romans, especially the poor, attending gladiator school, although it had its obvious dangers, also had its advantages.

Once in the arena, gladiators were expected to entertain the attending crowds who were keen to watch the spectacle. Two things were expected of gladiators: to fight well, and if necessary, to die well. Giving a good account of oneself was all important, because even if still alive after defeat a man could still lose his life, depending on how well the crowds felt he had fought. A 'thumbs up' from the masses ensured he lived to fight another day ...

Gladiatorial games lasted for almost 1,000 years, and were most popular between the first century BC and the second century AD. There were different types of gladiators and it didn't always appear that they were evenly matched when fighting in the arena. For example, two types of gladiators who couldn't have been more unevenly matched were the *retiarius* and the *secutor*. The former were traditionally smaller men, who wore no helmets and had minimal armour and equipment. For protection they only had a sleeve of armour which covered their left arm and shoulder. Their weaponry consisted of a large throwing net, accompanied by a trident and a dagger. In contrast, the latter, against whom they were often pitted, were much larger men, heavily armoured and helmeted.

The gladiatorial aspect of Roman life was easy to maintain as there was a readily available supply of suitable men. This was due in the main to the continuation of Rome's military success. Whereas all previously captured enemy combatants would usually be put to the sword, the bigger, fitter and stronger ones were sent to Rome to be trained as gladiators, and perhaps one day even earn their freedom. They were certainly allowed to keep their prize money and gifts, which could be substantial and include properties as well as cash.

In the first century AD, records exist that show there were even female gladiators, but as Roman morals directed that all gladiators were to be drawn from the lowest social classes of society, any such women are therefore likely to have been foreign slaves.

Gladiatorial games were grand affairs, usually put on for political reasons, which had the added bonus of keeping the common man and woman in a positive frame of mind, meaning there was less chance of them ever being rebellious towards the state. The games usually began after lunch with each bout or match lasting between ten and fifteen minutes, although they sometimes lasted for up to twenty. Regardless of how long the bouts took, the afternoon would usually see a maximum of about fifteen to twenty contests. Strange as celebrating the brutal and macabre deaths of a group of strangers might seem today, it was what passed for entertainment in Roman times, as well as being an equivalent of duelling of its day.

Trained gladiators were expected to adhere to specific rules of engagement. Combats between such men were usually overseen by a referee, known as a *summa rudis*, and sometimes an assistant. Both men had a long wooden staff which they used to separate the gladiators on occasions, during what might be deemed an important stage of the match. With most referees being retired gladiators, it provided an assurance that contests would be conducted as fairly as they possibly could. This included bouts even being stopped to provide gladiators with the opportunity for a rest, refreshment, and even a rub down because of the heat of the weather. Some of the bigger and grander events would be accompanied by music, sometimes even playing in time with each blow of a gladiator's sword.

A match, or a bout, was won when one gladiator either forced his opponent into submission, or killed him outright. A gladiator could eventually win his freedom in the arena. This was rare, but did happen, although it could take anywhere between three and five years before a gladiator had acquired himself a sufficiently good enough reputation to be even considered for such an event to take place. The official notification that such an achievement had been earned came in the form of a wooden sword called a *rudis*. Once presented with it, a man had his freedom and was no longer required to fight as a gladiator. Such an award was also possible if a gladiator gave an extraordinary performance in the arena, or did something that had never been seen before. In such rare occasions freedom could be earned immediately.

The period of history that is referred to as Imperial Rome lasted from 27 BC to AD 476. The first emperor of that era was Augustus Caesar, who ruled until his death in AD 14, and came to power after his great-uncle, Julius Caesar, had been assassinated. It was during this time that the sparing of a defeated gladiator's life, or *missio*, became what might be described as more commonplace. This was particularly the case if the crowds deemed it right that the life of a defeated gladiator should be saved, as it was a sure-fire way for an emperor to lose popularity with the people by going against their wishes. This in itself showed just how fragile the life and reign of an emperor could be.

The arena was in some respects a strange place for an emperor, for here was a man who had so much power, he determined if somebody lived or died, he could do whatever it was he wanted to in all aspects of life, and often did. By way of example, Emperor Caligula, who reigned between AD 37 and 41, was recorded by history as being a combination of cruel, sadistic, extravagant and a sexual pervert. But regardless of who was emperor at any given time, annoying the masses at an arena event could signify the beginning of the end for him. The emperors Caligula and Claudius, maybe in attempts to show who wielded the right of supreme power, had on more than one occasion gone against the wishes of the people, and refused to spare the lives of popular defeated gladiators, ultimately resulting in their own popularity declining amongst the masses. Somewhat of an own goal.

It was during the reign of Emperor Augustus that the number of events staged across the Roman Empire's amphitheatres increased dramatically, and with an estimation of there having been as many as 400 arenas, there was the potential for a large number of events taking place throughout the year. One of the obvious problems with this was the age old issue of supply and demand. With so many events taking place, there simply weren't enough gladiators to go round. This is possibly why the use of *missio* became more widespread.

Say for argument's sake that each amphitheatre put on just three events a year, remembering of course that some would continue for days and weeks at a time, that equates to approximately 1,200 events. This meant that on any day of the year there could be at least three events taking place, with up to 100 gladiators required at each of them. Add to this the equation that most gladiators fought in in no more than three or four events a year, it is easy to understand that there wasn't an exhaustive supply of gladiators to go round.

The other aspect of gladiators, their numbers and their training, was control. It didn't take a genius to work out the inherent dangers of having large numbers of gladiators, housed and living within society, especially in the very heart of Rome, without any controls. Before the Spartacus revolt, which began in 73 BC, most if not all gladiator schools were privately owned, where the only real pre-requisite was possessing sufficient wealth to be able to afford to keep and run such schools.

There was such a school in Capua, some 15 miles north of Naples, and owned by Gnaeus Cornelius Lentulus Batiatus, of whom history has not recorded anything of great note. In 73 BC, a group of slave-gladiators, led by the Thracian slave gladiator Spartacus, and which also included noted gladiators, Crixus, Gannicus, Castus and Oenomaus, took it upon themselves to escape from the school in a bid for freedom. Their actual reason for escaping is unclear and without any available documentation to be able to prove a definitive answer, the reason will always remain pure guesswork. But there are limits as to why they would have chosen to escape, such as freedom, a desire to put an end to slavery, or the intention of attempting to overthrow Rome.

A brief look at what is known about Spartacus shows that he was a heavily built gladiator known as a *murmillo*. Such gladiators carried a large oblong shield, known as a *scutum*, more commonly associated with that used by a soldier of the Roman army. The sword used by a *murmillo* had a straight blade length of about 18 inches, and was known as a *gladius*, which was also the primary weapon of choice of soldiers of the Roman army.

The slave revolt, which included a couple of notable victories over Roman forces, finally came to an end in 71 BC, when Spartacus and his followers were finally defeated by Marcus Licinius Crassus, a Roman general and politician, and his army of some 40,000 Roman soldiers, at the Battle of the Silarius River, in southern Campania, Italy.

A costly lesson had been learnt, and with this in mind, during the late Roman Republican era there was a fear that similar events could easily be repeated if controls weren't brought in concerning the keeping and owning of gladiators, as well as where the schools could be located. By the time of the Roman Emperor Domitian, who ruled between AD 81 and 96, nearly all gladiator schools were under state control. The city of Rome had four such schools, the *Ludus Magnus*, which was by far the biggest and most important, housing up to as many as 2,000 gladiators, the *Ludus Dacicus, Ludus Gallicus,* and the *Ludus Matutinus.* The latter was specifically for the training of *bestiarii*: gladiators who fought against wild animals, usually lions, tigers and bears.

Well-known gladiators

Tetraites was a well-known and popular gladiator of ancient Rome, who was much respected by the people. As with many of his contemporaries, few of his fights were documented, or if they were, the records didn't survive, which means that not much is actually known about him. His fame appears to have originated from a victory over a fellow gladiator, Prudes. It must have been an epic contest as both of their names have been found depicted on Roman-made glass vessels in France, England and Hungary.

It would appear that Tetraites, who attended the same gladiator school as Crixus and Spartacus at Capula, was killed in the arena during a 'games', some time before the gladiators' revolt of 73 BC.

Tetraites was also mentioned in graffiti discovered in Pompeii in 1817, which in itself is of massive historical importance. It is known that the eruption of Mount Vesuvius took place in AD 79, therefore we know for sure that Tetraites was alive some time before that date. What cannot be ascertained is how old the graffiti about Tetraites was.

Spiculus fought as a gladiator in the first century AD. Rumours have it that he was good friends with the Emperor Nero. If that is true, how that came to be is unclear. It can only be surmised that Nero was impressed by his prowess in the ring and took a shine to him. The friendship was such that Nero rewarded Spiculus extremely well for his victories in the arena, giving him his freedom, palaces, and riches beyond his wildest dreams, even with a touch of irony when he was given a number of slaves to cater for his every need. He was made a Roman citizen of high social rank, which for a man who had been a gladiator, was a real transformation of a position in society.

As with many of the gladiators, not much has been recorded about the early life of Spiculus, because at the time he simply wasn't that important. It was only as his reputation increased that his fame and popularity made him relevant to write about. But the scribes of the day had to be extremely mindful of what they wrote and how much detail they recorded, because no emperor wanted to be overshadowed by a mere gladiator, who was far lower down the social ladder than they were. The last thing that a scribe wanted to do was to annoy his emperor – that is if he valued his life.

As for Nero, he met his end when a plot was put in place to overthrow him. Amongst those involved in the plot were members of his own Praetorian Guards. One man who did stay loyal to him was Spiculus, but both men died; Nero by the hands of one of his own servants as he didn't have the stomach to take his own life. As for Spiculus, he was reported killed by an anti-Nero mob.

Hermes is an example of the names gladiators either chose for themselves or had chosen for them. As followers of Greek Mythology will no doubt know, Hermes is a deity in the religion of Ancient Greece, and is considered to be a herald of the gods, as well as the protector of travellers, thieves, merchants and orators. He also moves between the worlds of the living and the dead, and is a soul guide into the afterlife.

Priscus and **Verus** are always spoken about in the same sentence because of the mammoth fight which they put on the first day of the games celebrating the opening day of the Flavian Amphitheatre of Rome, more commonly known as the Colosseum, as an arena. The creation of the Colosseum certainly impressed the masses and helped raise Emperor

Titus's popularity amongst the people. Intended or otherwise, it was quite possibly one of the best things that Titus did throughout his entire reign.

As was shown with the contest between Priscus and Verus, not all gladiatorial fights ended in a death, but these were exceptional cases. The crowds at such events would usually have a favourite in most of the fights, so for both men to live and be awarded a *rudis* by the emperor, it must have been an extraordinary fight on the part of both of them. What was unusual in this case was that both combatants were declared the victor by Emperor Titus.

The following was written about the fight:

> As Priscus and Verus drew out the contest and the struggle between the pair long stood equal, shouts loud and often sought discharge for the combatants. But Titus obeyed his own law, the law was that the bout go on without shield until a finger be raised. What he could do, he did, often giving dishes and presents. But an end to the event strife was found: equal they fought, equal they yielded. To both, Titus sent wooden swords and to both, palms. Thus valor and skill had their reward. This has happened under no Prince but you, Titus: two fought and both won.

The Colosseum was so advanced in its structure that it was possible to stage a sea battle by flooding the lower part of the arena. It must have been an extremely spectacular sight.

Not much was expected of **Marcus Attilius** as a gladiator, other than to maybe die as honourably as he could in the arena. But he turned out to be something of a force to be reckoned with. One of the aspects of gladiatorial fights was that the match up of opponents was usually done fairly, so that the crowd at least had the opportunity of seeing a fight between two men who were relatively evenly matched size-wise as well in experience. On the day of Marcus Attilius's first fight, the 'rule book' seems to have been thrown out of the window because he was pitched against 'the tall, powerfully built and extremely experienced' Hilarus, who had won the special distinction of a wreath no fewer than thirteen times. The presumption being that maybe the authorities wanted a quick death for Attilius, and at the same time providing another easy victory for Hilarus, but matters didn't go the way they were intended, with Attilius winning the fight – to almost everybody's surprise.

Shimon Ben Lakish was Jewish and born somewhere around 200 BC, in Syria Palaestina, which at the time was a Roman province.

It appears that Lakish was large in size, more corpulent than muscular, but still useful enough to make his size a useful advantage rather than a hindrance. One of his endearing traits was his desire to continually learn and improve himself. By all accounts, he didn't die in the arena, but of a sudden and unknown illness.

Carpophorus is another person who is often mentioned when the names of great gladiators are spoken about. However, he wasn't even a gladiator, but a *venator*, which in layman's terms means that he fought animals for money and glory.

He came to prominence during the games of AD 80, which had been ordered by the Emperor Titus to help celebrate the finishing of the building of the Colosseum in Rome. His reputation appears to have been earned because he managed to do nothing other than kill a large number of animals.

Most gladiators had a name that conjured up a combination of fear, aggression and respect. In those terms **Crixus** was no different, but his name (which was Gaulish), actually translated into nothing more frightening than 'one with curly hair'. However, the very mention of his name would have no doubt placed the fear of God in most of his opponents. How he became enslaved and forced to fight as a gladiator isn't recorded, although it is more than likely he was a captured enemy soldier.

He was a friend of Spartacus, and one of those who escaped from the gladiator school at Capula in 73 BC. Although he enjoyed some initial successes in the fighting immediately after the escape, he and his army, which it is estimated numbered some 30,000 men, decided to break away from the main rebel army. There could be a number of reasons why this took place, but two obvious ones come to the fore as strong possibilities. It may have been for strategic reasons decided upon by Spartacus and the other rebel leaders, or there could have been a disagreement as what was the best course of action to take next, with Spartacus wanting to escape, whilst Crixus wanted to carry on fighting in the belief that he and his men could defeat whatever armies Rome decided to throw at them.

In 72 BC, Crixus and his men encountered a Roman army near Mount Gargano in southern Italy, who were under the command of the Roman Consul, Lucius Gellius Publicola, Crixus and his men were all killed. Spartacus is rumoured to have taken the news of his friend's death badly.

Flamma was a good example of an age for a gladiators. A captured Syrian soldier forced into becoming a gladiator, he was one of the most respected, yet his real name isn't recorded. Flamma, meaning flame, was the name that he chose for fighting in the arena. At the time of his death he was aged 30, by which time he had fought a total of thirty-four duels. Although that may sound a lot, it was over a period of more than twelve years, so not even three times a year. In some respects he was fortunate to still be alive as he won only twenty-one of his fights, with another nine being draws, and the other four ending in defeats, three of which saw his life being spared, but in his final fight he was killed in battle. Remarkably, Flamma had been awarded the *rudis* at least four times, but decided to carry on fighting as a gladiator on each occasion, adding a certain poignancy to his death.

If one were to ask the question of followers of the history of ancient Rome, who was the most famous gladiator of all time, a large number of them would reply, **Spartacus**. Why was he so famous, or rather notorious? To a large extent his fame was derived from the gladiator uprisings in 73 BC, when a number of them escaped from the gladiator school of Batiatus in Capua. Over the following two years many slaves joined Spartacus's army, which at its peak is estimated to have been as large as 100,000 in number.

In the battles that ensued, Spartacus and his armies won a number of resounding victories against Roman forces. It just shouldn't have happened: a slave army up against the finest, best-trained, and most professional soldiers the world had ever seen, and they defeated them, one after the other. To say that it was an embarrassment for Rome was an understatement.

It was only when Marcus Licinius Crassus decided to intervene in events that Spartacus and his slave army were eventually defeated. At the time he was one of the wealthiest men in the whole of Rome. Pliny the Elder, who was a military man, a philosopher and author, estimated that Crassus's net worth was equal to the total annual budget of the Roman treasury.

Although Emperor Commodus is frequently recorded on the list of the most famous gladiators, he wasn't a gladiator. As his title suggests, he was an emperor – and not a particularly good one. One of his main traits was vanity, although his biggest was his ego. He needed the thrill of the arena, but his own opponents were either tethered animals, or feeble individuals who were only armed with wooden swords. Putting it bluntly, he was a joke. The only one who didn't seem to understand that, was Commodus himself.

There was a subtle irony in that Commodus desired to be a great gladiator, yet despite the glamour that surrounded them, they were considered to have a very low social status in the eyes of the upper classes. They were only popular in the eyes of the masses, who I have absolutely no doubt would have seen right through him.

CHAPTER THREE

Scandinavian Holmgang

Holmgang was a duel that was practised by early medieval Scandinavians as an acceptable, and more importantly, legal way of settling disputes between two people.

The difference, if there is one, between a *Holmgang* and a European or early American-style duel, is that in the former, social status didn't matter, anybody could challenge anybody, whereas the European/American versions were much more class-orientated and the sole domain of the upper classes of society.

The reasons for *Holmgang* varied. It could be evoked because of honour, disputes over property, general disagreements, restitution of debts owed, to help a female relative, or to avenge a friend. Once somebody had been challenged to a *Holmgang*, it had to take place within three to seven days. If after agreeing to take part, a man failed to turn up, the other man was deemed just, in either his allegations or denial. The absentee could also be sentenced to 'outlawry' as he was unable or unwilling to defend the allegations which had been made against him, and he was deemed to have no honour. This meant that he was now outside the protection of the law and anybody could persecute or kill him, without any worry of themselves being prosecuted. It was an extremely harsh sentence.

To ensure that a bigger and stronger man, who was possibly also battle-hardened, didn't challenge somebody to *Holmgang*, a capable warrior could volunteer to fight in the place of a relative or friend, who was obviously going to be outclassed by his challenger.

A thirteenth-century document from Vastergotland, Sweden, provides the rules for a *Holmgang* to take place:

> If someone speaks insults to another man, they shall meet where three roads meet. If he who has spoken comes and not the insulted one, then he shall be as he's been called: no right to swear oaths, no right to bear witness, may it concern man or woman.
>
> If the insulted one comes and not he who has spoken, then he shall cry '*Nioongr!*' three times and make a mark in the ground, and he is worse who spoke what he dared not keep.
>
> Now both meet fully armed: if the insulted one falls, the compensation is half a weregild [man price]; if he who has spoken falls, insults are the worst, the tongue the head's bane, he shall lie in a field of no compensation.

Although there were rules, they weren't universal and would vary from location to location and over time. But on each occasion the rules of an individual *Holmgang* would be agreed between the two duellists, and these would be read out loud by the challenger before the duel took place. This would include such aspects as the weapons to be used, what constituted a defeat, or a forfeiture, and what was at stake. Sometimes this could be everything that the loser owned.

Over time, *Holmgangs* became more ritualistic, similar to a European duel, whereby it was more about turning up than actually killing or wounding an opponent. As I have written about elsewhere in this book, there are many accounts where one man would intentionally miss his opponent and in return he would do the same.

As *Holmgangs* were legal in Scandinavian law, killing an opponent in one of these duels didn't constitute a murder. One aspect of the spectacle was that the contest took place within a very confined space, and the way it was set out openly encouraged each competitor to fight as close to their opponent as possible. It was like 'milling' in the army where two men stand toe to toe and punch each other without moving backwards or out of the way of incoming blows. The area for a *Holmgang* was no bigger than the size of an ox hide stretched out and pegged into the ground, with a further 3ft outside it, split at 1ft distances. The competitors had to fight within these borders. Stepping outside of the borders could lead to forfeiture.

A *Holmgang* began with the challenger striking the first blow and thereafter each man took turns in striking his opponent, although each man had a shield to protect himself, which could be replaced if broken by a strike, but this was usually restricted to an agreed number. The winner was the first man to draw blood from his opponent, but most wounds resulted in a man sustaining more than a mere scratch.

Holmgangs were often abused by some as a means of claiming another man's land, property and woman. The men who did this were in effect professional duellists; it was how they made their living, albeit with a devastating outcome for their innocent victims. It was largely because of this misuse that the *Holmgang* began to be outlawed throughout Scandinavia at the beginning of the eleventh century.

CHAPTER FOUR

America Before the Wild West

The most famous duel in American history took place on 11 July 1804, between Alexander Hamilton, a leading Federalist and former secretary of the American treasury, and Aaron Burr, who at the time was serving as vice president under Thomas Jefferson. The two men met at the duelling grounds near Weehawken, New Jersey, the same spot where Hamilton's son had died defending his father's honour in November 1801. The loss of his son had inspired Hamilton to denounce duelling and lend his voice to the growing movement against its practice.

It appears that the conflict between the two men began as far back as 1791, when Philip Schuyler, Hamilton's father-in-law, lost his position on the US Senate to Burr.

In a letter dated 4 January 1801, which Hamilton wrote to his good friend James McHenry, his contempt for Burr was evident. The letter included the following:

> Nothing has given me so much chagrin as the intelligence that the Federal Party were thinking seriously of supporting Mr Burr for President. I should consider the execution of the plan as devoting

the country and signing their own death warrant. Mr Burr will probably make stipulations, but he will laugh in his sleeve while he makes them and will break them the first moment it may serve his purpose.

Whilst he had been a member of the legislature, Hamilton had accused Burr of corruptly serving the interests of the Holland Land Company, which was a syndicate of thirteen Dutch investors from Amsterdam who bought up land in New York State and Pennsylvania.

Hamilton had come to detest Burr, whom he thought of as an opportunist. During the 1804 elections to become Governor of New York, he had campaigned against him and must have derived great pleasure and satisfaction when Burr failed to win the position, losing out to fellow Democratic-Republican, Morgan Lewis. The election saw Burr backed by members of the Federalist Party, who wanted New York to join the New England States in an independent confederation. This was something that was strongly opposed by the party's national leader, Alexander Hamilton.

Burr felt slighted by not winning the election to become the Governor of New York, and to an extent blamed Hamilton for his defeat. Ironically, the reason he had attempted to gain the position was because he knew that President Thomas Jefferson intended to drop Burr as his vice president in the 1804 presidential elections.

Although his political reputation wasn't exactly in tatters, his pride had most definitely been dented. He determined that he could go a long way to restoring his reputation by challenging Hamilton to a duel or, as it was called at the time, an 'affair of honour'.

Hamilton had been the second in several previous duels, and had also been involved in more than a dozen affairs of honour dating back to 1779.

The build up to the fatal duel appears to have originated from a letter which appeared in the *Albany Register* newspaper, dated 24 April 1804. Its author was Charles D. Cooper, a Democratic-Republican, physician and lawyer, and he had originally sent it to Hamilton's father-in-law, former senator Philip Schuyler. The letter included the following sentence:

> General Hamilton and Judge Kent have declared in substance that they looked upon Mr Burr to be a dangerous man, and one who ought not to be trusted with the reins of government.

Cooper added that he could describe in great detail, 'a still more despicable opinion which General Hamilton has expressed of Mr Burr at a political dinner'.

Once Burr became aware of Cooper's letter in the newspaper for all to see, he had no option but to respond. He sent a letter to Hamilton via a trusted friend, William P. van Ness, which highlighted his dislike of the words 'more despicable', demanding 'a prompt and unqualified acknowledgement or denial of the use of any expression which would warrant the assertion of Dr Cooper'.

Hamilton sent a reply to Burr explaining that he couldn't be held responsible for an interpretation by Cooper of what he had said, but more to the point, neither did he disagree or distance himself from the comments. He accepted the consequences if Burr remained unsatisfied at his response. This led to Burr sending another letter to Hamilton, which was once again delivered by his good friend van Ness. In essence it said that regardless of a man's political persuasion, honour and decorum should still prevail between gentlemen. Hamilton replied that he had 'no other answer to give than that which has already been given'.

The communication between the two men wasn't going anywhere, and certainly not forward. Hamilton's response forced Burr's hand to a large degree: after all, this was about honour. He had been disrespected in the press, concerning allegations which he refuted and since he received no kind of apology or retraction, he had no option other than to formally challenge Hamilton to a duel. This also forced Hamilton's hand. Having made allegations against Burr, which the latter considered to be of a slanderous nature, that he either couldn't or wouldn't recant, if he backed away from a formal challenge his character and good name would be left in ruins. It was a situation of his own making and he had to accept the challenge whether he wanted to or not.

Besides his life, Hamilton and his family had much to lose. As a husband and father, he was placing his family's welfare at stake by going ahead with the duel; all because of honour. In his head it must have been a battle between morals: family and religion on the one hand; the codes of honour and politics on the other. Only he could decide which was more important.

The day of the duel finally arrived. Both men left their Manhattan homes early in the morning and sailed in separate boats slowly and quietly across the Hudson River until they reached Weehawken in New Jersey. Even though it was by then already illegal in both New York and New Jersey, Weehawken had become a popular location for duelling, probably because the New Jersey authorities were less inclined to prosecute those who took part in such events than their associates in New York.

Between 1700 and 1845 there were a total of eighteen known duels at Weehawken, including one in 1801 that resulted in the death of Hamilton's eldest son Philip, who was shot by New York lawyer, George Eacker, when he was just 19 years old. William Peter van Ness, Burr's second, along with Burr and his supporters, arrived first at 6.30 am, with Hamilton and his team arriving just before 7 am. There is a lot of conjecture about what transpired; letters that were subsequently written about the events and interpretations of what Burr and Hamilton said but actually meant. It isn't clear who fired first and if either man intentionally missed or fired with intent to kill the other man, but simply missed in the attempt. However, all present agreed that only two shots were fired.

Hamilton took his shot and missed (either he was a poor shot or it was intentional). Burr then took aim and struck Hamilton in the stomach above the right hip. It transpired that the lead ball ricocheted off Hamilton's third false rib, fracturing it and causing considerable damage to some of his internal organs, particularly his liver and diaphragm, before lodging in his first or second lumbar vertebra. He died from his wounds the following day at the home of the prominent New York City banker William Bayard Jr. in the affluent area of Greenwich Village. Before he died, he met with his wife and children, along with a number of friends and family. He was buried in the Trinity Churchyard Cemetery in Manhattan, New York.

Rather than restoring his reputation, the duel and the killing of Hamilton ruined Burr. The nation was outraged that such an eminent member of society had been killed in this way. The Federalist Party was greatly affected and weakened by Hamilton's death. Public opinion didn't just turn against Burr, American society did.

Burr was arrested and charged with murder in both New York and New Jersey, but neither case ended up going to trial. But that wasn't the end of the matter. Political forces were in play and those pulling the strings were like a dog with a bone, they simply weren't going to let the matter go away; after all Burr was the vice president of America. In November 1804, a grand jury in Bergen County, New Jersey indicted him for murder, but after a motion from Colonel Aaron Ogden, a member of the New Jersey General Assembly, the Supreme Court of New Jersey quashed the case against Burr and he left court a free and innocent man. On his release, he went and stayed on a plantation on St Simons Island in Georgia, before eventually returning to Washington to finish his term of office as vice president.

Andrew Jackson, who was the seventh US President (prior to which time he had served in the United States army, reaching the rank of general), actually fought in two duels. The first took place on 30 May 1806, when he fought Charles Dickinson, a well-known duellist of the day, and an expert marksman.

Dickinson moved to Tennessee sometime around the beginning of the nineteenth century, becoming a successful horse breeder and plantation owner. It was also where he met, fell in love with, and married the daughter of Captain Joseph Erwin.

The events which unfolded, resulting in the duel taking place between the two men, started in 1805 with an argument over a bet on a horse race made by a friend of Andrew Jackson's, which had been handled by Captain Erwin. The original problem hadn't involved either of the men who had the initial dispute.

Erwin and Jackson owned horses, Ploughboy and Truxton, which they had arranged to race against each other for a purse of $2,000 to be paid by the loser, with an agreement that if for any reason either horse was unable to race, the owner of that horse would pay the other $800 in recompense. Sod's law being what it is, Erwin's horse, Ploughman, became lame and had to be withdrawn from the race, causing a disagreement between Erwin and Jackson as to how the $800 should be paid. This in turn became a heated argument, although matters eventually calmed down and Erwin paid Jackson the $800.

Dickinson became involved when he heard that a friend of Jackson had been bad mouthing Erwin in relation to the $800 payment he had owed to Jackson. On hearing this, Dickinson sent a friend of his, Thomas Swann, to intervene on his behalf to find out exactly what Jackson had been saying about Erwin's conduct in relation to the payment of the $800. Whatever Swann reported to Dickinson, and whether his words were correct or mistaken, is unclear, and to a degree is now somewhat irrelevant. But it made matters even worse.

Sometime later Jackson saw Swann in Winn's Tavern in Nashville. The men exchanged words, which resulted in Jackson striking Swann with his cane and calling him a 'stupid meddler'.

Rather than calming down and discussing the matter like gentlemen, both parties became more entrenched in the stance they had taken, which resulted in the situation quickly escalating out of control. Dickinson wrote to Jackson calling him a 'coward and an equivocator'. Swann turned to the local newspaper, the *Nashville Review* to vent his anger and displeasure at Jackson's treatment of him, calling him a 'coward'. Jackson replied in kind, put pen to paper and posted it to the same newspaper, who were only too happy to print its contents, part of which referred to Swann being a 'lying valet for a worthless, drunkard, blackguard', the blackguard in question being Dickinson.

The argument continued with the possibility of an agreeable resolution to the situation becoming more and more unlikely. Looking at it through the eyes of history, it doesn't even appear that either side was actively trying to resolve the matter. Each had simply become intent at throwing verbal insults at the other, which ultimately was only ever going to finish one way. Maybe that was the intention by at least one side all along?

Word of Jackson's comments reached Dickinson, who on hearing them on his return from a trip to New Orleans in May 1806 upped the ante somewhat when he published a statement in the same newspaper, in which he called Jackson a 'worthless scoundrel, a poltroon [wretched coward] and a coward'.

Jackson wrote to Dickinson demanding satisfaction for his insults.

If the two men were to settle their differences through a duel, they had a problem as duelling had been illegal in Tennessee since around the turn of the century, although in 1806 it was extremely difficult to be extradited across state borders. After giving the matter some consideration, it was agreed that they would face each other in Adairville, Kentucky, about 125 miles away from Nashville, but just across the county line with Tennessee.

Jackson was well aware of Dickinson's reputation as an excellent shot, so employing some of his military skills, he came up with a plan of action along with his friend and second, General Thomas Overton.

Sometimes on a battlefield the best results are achieved when the commanding officer throws the rule book out of the window, basically ignoring laid down, successful and proven tactics. Despite the obvious threat that Dickinson posed, Jackson and Overton agreed that they should let Dickinson fire first in the hope that in his urgency he would miss. Although there was a sound logic to their thought process, if the two men got it wrong it would result in Jackson being wounded sufficiently badly, if not killed, before he could take his own shot.

For the plan to be successful, Overton, as Jackson's second, needed to win the toss so that he was in control of the call to begin the duel. The plan was for him to first ask Jackson, 'Gentleman, are you ready?' He would then ask Dickinson the same question, and after he had replied or nodded his readiness, Overton would immediately say the word 'fire', in an attempt to cause Dickinson to fire first, and possibly more quickly than he would have naturally done so. This is exactly what happened.

True to his reputation, Dickinson's aim was good, his round striking Jackson in the chest. As if by a miracle, not only was he not mortally wounded as might have been expected by such a shot, but he even managed to remain on his feet. Dickinson was now in an extremely precarious position, because under the rules of duelling, and to retain his honour, he couldn't move his position. Jackson took his time, calmed himself down, and despite his injuries managed to retain his composure. He aim and pulled the trigger of his pistol, but the weapon didn't discharge, as the hammer stopped at half cock, so he drew it back, took aim once again and fired. His shot struck Dickinson square in the chest knocking him to the ground, where he bled to death.

Luckily for Jackson, because of the stance he would have taken to fire, sideways on, and being right-handed, his heart was in the part of his body furthest away from any shot that struck him. Dickinson's shot initially struck a brass button on Jackson's coat, which deflected the bullet slightly, and undoubtedly also reducing its speed, albeit fractionally. The round also struck a number of his ribs, slowing it down some more, and it finally came to rest just a few inches from his heart. Because of its proximity to Jackson's heart, it was deemed to be too tricky to remove the bullet, so it remained lodged in his body for the rest of his life.

There was some controversy surrounding Jackson's fatal shot on Dickinson. Initially there was some confusion amongst the seconds on both sides. In the rules of duelling, if a man pulled the trigger on his pistol, and the hammer fell completely but the weapon failed to discharge, this was included as a shot, but in Jackson's case, when he pulled the hammer on his pistol it only went to half cock meaning that he was still able to take his shot.

Jackson could have also been chivalrous and fired into the ground, the air or aimed at Dickinson's legs, which would have meant that both men's honour had been satisfied, but in his mind there was no doubt that Dickinson had tried his best to kill him, so he responded in kind.

It is said that the duel, and possibly his decision to take his shot rather than be magnanimous, harmed his reputation. But it didn't stop him from becoming a US Senator for Tennessee between 1823 and 1825, or the seventh US President on 4 March 1829, a position he held for eight years until the same date in 1837. He died on 8 June 1845, aged 78, in Nashville, Tennessee.

On 22 September 1842, a duel was planned to take place in Illinois between an Illinois state legislator, and a state auditor by the name of James Shields, who during the Mexican-American War of 1846–48, served in the US army as a brigadier general, serving with distinction whilst being wounded twice. He left the army in 1848 and was appointed by the Senate as the first governor of Oregon, a post which he declined, taking up the position of Senator of Minnesota instead. He rejoined the army during the American Civil War of 1861–65, serving as an officer in the Union Army. At the Battle of Kernstown on 23 March 1862, in Frederick County and Winchester, Virginia, his troops inflicted the only tactical defeat of Confederate General 'Stonewall' Jackson, of the entire American Civil War.

The name of the state legislator, the other protagonist in the duel, was a 33-year-old Abraham Lincoln who, in 1861, would become the sixteenth US President.

Lincoln and his fiancée, Mary Todd, whom he married in November 1842, wrote a number of unflattering letters about Shields in a local newspaper. In response, an annoyed and angry Shields challenged Lincoln to a duel, which he accepted. The duel was set to take place on 22 September 1842, but thankfully for the American nation, the men's seconds intervened and persuaded them to resolve the matter amicably. Ironically, when Lincoln was president during the American Civil War, he was Shield's superior and the two men went on to become good friends. How different things might have been for America if the duel had gone ahead and Lincoln had been killed.

CHAPTER FIVE

Gunfights of the Wild West

◈

On 13 September 1859, what was subsequently referred to as 'the last notable American duel' took place between David C. Broderick and David S. Terry. Now this was no ordinary gunfight between a couple of gunslinging cowboys, this was between two of the most esteemed men in American society.

Broderick was a United States senator and Terry was the ex-chief justice of the Supreme Court of California and for many years the men had been friends as well as political allies. A problem arose between the two men because Broderick was an abolitionist, who wanted to see slavery ended, whilst Terry supported slavery. Unfortunately their political differences not only ruined their friendship but also caused bitter resentment between the two men, and resulted in them taking part in a duel at a location near Lake Merced in San Francisco.

Besides the death of Broderick, the duel resulted in a change of public opinion in relation to the whole subject of duelling and all that it stood for. Soon afterwards, most states brought in legislation to try and prevent its continuation.

As well as being close friends, the pair were both Democrats and politically had the utmost respect for each other. But that all changed when Terry was up for re-election as the chief justice of the Supreme Court in California, but lost his position. Rightly or wrongly, Terry saw the reason behind his unexpected defeat being because of his connection with Broderick, who was leading an anti-slavery campaign, unpopular with a large number of other Democrats. On the other side of the coin, Broderick believed that many of Terry's closest political allies were trying to undermine his campaign.

Each blamed the other for his woes, and accusation and counter-accusation became the norm between the two men.

How the relationship between two men of such high social status descended into an acrimonious situation, where one of them ended up dead, seems incredible. At one point, the situation between them was so dire that Broderick said of his rival:

> I see that Terry has been abusing me. I now take back the remark I once made that he is the only honest judge in the Supreme Court. I was his friend when he was in need of friends, for which I am sorry. Had the vigilance committee disposed of him as they did of others, they would have done a righteous act.

As if the situation wasn't bad enough between the two men, it went from bad to worse when Terry tried to be re-nominated as a Supreme Court Justice. However, this wasn't allowed because of Broderick's support of the Lecompton Constitution. Terry wasn't pleased and made no attempt at hiding his anger towards Broderick, accusing convention delegates in a speech in June 1859 in Sacramento, California, of following Broderick's orders.

The Lecompton Constitution of 1857 was one of four proposed constitutions for the state of Kansas, which had been drafted by pro-slavery advocates. The constitution included provisions for the protection of the state's slave owners, and excluded blacks who were free men from its Bill of Rights. To many people's surprise, on 4 January 1858, the Lecompton Constitution was resoundingly defeated by the majority of Kansas voters. Its rejection, and the subsequent admittance of Kansas into the Union as a free state, highlighted the irregular and fraudulent voting practices which had been deployed across Kansas, despite the efforts of some elements who tried to ensure that slavery was allowed throughout the state.

Broderick found out about Terry's speech in Sacramento two days after it had been made. His response was to call him a 'damned miserable ingrate'. As is quite often the case when one makes a glib comment out of anger, it is more than likely going to be heard by somebody who you either didn't realise was present, or if you did, you were unaware they weren't actually on your side. That was exactly the case with what Broderick said. One of Terry's supporters overheard Broderick's comment and informed Terry of what had been said. On 8 September 1859, Terry wrote the following letter to Broderick.

Hon. D. C. Broderick

Sir,

Some two months since at the public table of the International Hotel, in San Francisco, you saw fit to indulge in certain remarks concerning me, which were offensive in their nature. Before I had heard of the circumstance, your note of 20th of June, addressed to Mr. D. W. Perley, in which you declared that you would not respond to any call of a personal character during the political canvass just concluded, had been published.

I have, therefore, not been permitted to take any notice of those remarks until the expiration of the limit fixed by yourself. I now take the earliest opportunity to require of you a retraction of those remarks. This note will be handed to you by my friend, Calhoun Benham, Esq., who is acquainted with its contents, and will receive your reply.

D. S. Terry.

Intentionally or otherwise, Terry's letter was tantamount to challenging Broderick to a duel. His response in relation to the letter was to inform Terry that it was down to him to determine what statements of his he found offensive. Neither man would back down or change their chosen stance, which resulted in a duel being scheduled for 10 September 1859, but it had to be cancelled due to the intervention of the local constabulary. It eventually went ahead three days later, near Lake Merced. The agreed weapons of choice for both men were Belgian-made .58 calibre pistols, a model of gun that Terry was familiar with, but which Broderick wasn't. Both weapons had hair triggers, which meant they were liable to discharge at the slightest touch.

There was no interruption by the police on the second occasion and the duel went ahead as planned. It was Terry who fired the fatal shot, although Broderick wasn't killed outright, he died of his wounds three days later in hospital, on 16 September 1859. Political gain was certainly made out of Broderick's death. He became treated as a martyr for the cause in the fight against slavery, with his funeral becoming a catalyst for demonstrations of public support that San Francisco had never seen before. He was buried at the city's Lone Mountain Cemetery.

The authorities decided to arrest Terry on suspicion of murder. To this end, two detectives attended Terry's home with a warrant. As the two men got within about a hundred yards of the front of his house, a living room window was flung open and four shotguns were aimed in their direction. The men with their fingers on the triggers were Sheriff O'Neil, Calhoun Benham, Tom Hayes and David Terry. The two detectives identified themselves, stating that they had a warrant for Terry's arrest, but in return he stated that he was certain that he couldn't receive a fair trial and feared for his safety if he left at that time with the two detectives. He did, however, agree to surrender himself in Oakland three days later. The detectives now found themselves in rather a quandary as to what to do, but considering their options, they agreed to Terry's demands, knowing that he was too high profile an individual not to honour the agreement he had just made. They also knew that to try and carry out the arrest by pushing the matter would probably result in their deaths.

Terry kept to his word and handed himself into the authorities in Oakland three days later. The subsequent case was heard by Judge James Hardy in Marin County, having been moved there from San Francisco to countenance the alleged prejudice against Terry in the city. After hearing all the allegations and evidence, the case against Terry was thrown out, but he was indicted by the Grand Jury in San Mateo County. Once it had been pointed out that he had already been tried for the same offence, and without any new evidence it would be unfair to try him again, the case was dismissed.

In 1881, James O'Meara, who had been present when Broderick was shot, provided an eyewitness account of the duel. He wrote the following concerning Broderick:

> His rigor of frame was so intense that, in the effort to adjust his pistol to the required position, he was obliged to use his left hand to bring his right arm into proper form; and in the effort he also so swerved his whole body that his right leg was pressed out of place, downward and forward, out of line with the left leg, and his chest was thrown out and quartering toward his antagonist, so as to present a larger surface for the chance of a shot aimed at him. He held his pistol in vice-like grip; and his wrist, instead of being in condition for ease of motion, was as an iron bolt, to move only with and as rigidly as the arm. He seemed the impersonation of that order of courage which faces death without terror, which prefers doom to the reproach of fear.

Clearly such duels were fraught with danger for both the winner and the loser. For the man who lost, it could cost him his life, but even for the victor there was the likelihood of being dragged through the courts and the possibility that they would be found guilty of murder and be hung.

The famous cowboy known as **'Wild Bill' Hickok** was involved in a gunfight against **Davis Tutt**, a hardened gambler, in the town square of Springfield, Missouri, on **12 July 1865**. What makes this incident unique is it was the first ever one-on-one, quick-draw pistol duel in a public place. It is also one of the few recorded instances of such a duel.

The story of the duel between the two men was recorded in *Harper's Magazine,* a monthly magazine which covered topics such as literature, politics, culture, finance and the arts. The inclusion of the story about Hickok and Tutt, made Hickok famous across America, and somewhat of a folk hero.

Both men were gamblers and had been for many years, it was simply part and parcel of frequenting a saloon on a regular basis. They had, at one point, even been friends, despite the fact that during the American Civil War they had been on opposite sides: Hickok had served as a scout for the Union Army, whilst Tutt had been a private in the Confederate Army.

Davis Tutt had originally come from Marion County, Arkansas, where his family had been involved in the Tutt-Everett War, during which several of them had been killed. Tutt had moved north to Missouri after the end of the American Civil War. The Tutt-Everett War, also referred to as the Marion County War, lasted for six years between 1844 and 1850, politically a particularly highly charged era.

The background to the feud had political overtones to it as the Tutt family were ardent supporters of the Whig Party, whilst the Everett family were long standing supporters of the Democratic Party. The Tutt family had moved to Arkansas from Tennessee, and went on to become very influential in the Searcy County area of Arkansas. When there was talk about dividing the areas of Marion and Searcy, the Tutts were vehemently opposed to the idea.

The first record of any kind of aggression or violence between the two families came during a political debate in 1844, in the city of Yellville, in Marion County. Tensions ran high, leading to verbal threats and allegations on both sides, but before long the incident had degenerated into an all-out brawl, resulting in John Everett being struck with a bladed instrument, which left him with a very nasty head wound.

Over the following four years, a number of arguments took place between the feuding families, usually whenever they met in public. Family loyalty at these times usually dictated that words alone weren't sufficient to sate either side, resulting in fist fights and brawls.

On 9 October 1848, a gunfight took place in Yellville, which resulted in the death of John Everett. On 11 October 1848, the Everetts retaliated, not by shooting or killing one of the Tutts, but by killing two men, father and son, William and Lumis King, who were friends of the Tutts. Billy King (another son of William King) and a friend of his, known by the name of 'Cherokee' Bob, were both wounded in the same shooting but managed to escape. The situation between the two families took an interesting step when Ewell Everett was elected as the judge of Searcy County, whilst George Adams, a friend of the Tutts, became a constable. Neither appointment helped quash the tensions between the two families.

By July 1849, matters were so out of hand between the two families that Marion County sheriff, Jesse Mooney, a man with a fearful reputation due to having killed or captured several local men who had placed themselves above the law, organised a posse to bring an end to the feud once and for all. Things didn't quite go according to plan. Before Sheriff Mooney and his posse had left town, the Tutts and Everetts had gathered in Yellville. The Tutts were meeting in the town's saloon, whilst the Everetts had gathered in a building across the road after hearing of the Tutts meeting.

Despite Sheriff Mooney's attempts at keeping the peace and preventing both sides from getting at one another, a gunfight broke out. Sheriff Mooney and his posse, who were being completely ignored, were trapped in the middle. Even when the shooting finished (because both sides had run out of ammunition), the fighting didn't stop. The Tutts and Everetts rushed out into the street and carried on the fight with knifes and clubs.

By the time the fighting had finally finished, five men, Jack King, Bart Everett, Davis Tutt, Ben Tutt and Lunsford Tutt, lay dead in the street, whilst a number of others were wounded, including John Hurst, who had been shot in the leg whilst trying to protect Sheriff Mooney.

Returning to the story of Tutt and Hickok. Ironically Hickok had moved from Illinois, because he mistakenly believed he had killed a man in a drunken bar-room brawl.

Hickok and Tutt were already at loggerheads over women. It was rumoured that Tutt's unmarried sister had given birth to a child fathered by Hickok, whilst Tutt had been paying a lot of attention to Hickok's lady friend, Susana Moore.

But the rift between the two men finally came to a head on that fateful day in Springfield, Missouri on 12 July 1865. Hickok had been playing poker against several other local gamblers in the Lyon House Hotel. Although Tutt wasn't one of them, he was there. He even handed over money to some of those taking part in the game and offered them advice on how to beat Hickok. Despite this, Hickok was still winning and was up by some $200, which today (2021) would have a value of somewhere in the region of $3,340, a substantial sum of money for most. The irony of this for Tutt was the more money that Hickok won from the other players, the more he lost, as in essence it was the money he had loaned the other players that Hickok was winning.

In an effort to annoy Hickok, or at least make him lose his concentration, Tutt reminded Hickok that he owed him $40 in relation to the sale of a horse. Unperturbed, Hickok calmly counted out $40 dollars and handed it over. Still Tutt wouldn't let matters drop and shouted out that he owed him a further $35 from a previous poker game, which Hickok challenged, replying that the sum owed was in fact only $25.

Tutt certainly felt safe in his goading of Hickok, possibly because of the large number of his friends and associates who were also present at the Lyon House. On the table in front of him, Hickok had one of his most prized possessions, a gold pocket watch. It was a routine of his when he was playing poker. Knowing how much the watch meant to Hickok, and feeling braver than he possibly should have, Tutt grabbed the watch saying that he would keep the watch as collateral until Hickok paid him the full $35 owed. Hickok was far from impressed with Tutt snatching his watch, but he was also fully aware that Tutt had a large number of associates around him, and to challenge him then and there wouldn't have been sensible. He left his gun in its holster and resisted the strong desire to retrieve his watch by the use of violence, settling instead for a request for Tutt to be kind enough to put his pocket watch back on the table. Tutt looked at Hickok, turned, and strode out of the hotel with Hickok's pocket watch in his possession.

By taking the pocket watch, Tutt placed Hickok in a difficult position. He couldn't react to being publicly humiliated by Tutt grabbing his gold watch as he otherwise would have. For Tutt to say that he was taking it as collateral for an unpaid debt from a man who earned his living playing poker could also imply that he was so short of funds that he didn't have sufficient money to pay his dues. For Hickok to ignore the slur completely, whether, intended or otherwise, could have resulted in there being nobody in Springfield willing to play against him anymore, ending his only known source of income.

The taking of the watch was also the catalyst for Tutt's acquaintances to start baiting Hickok about his watch to see if they could get him angry enough to go for his gun so they could shoot him, but he didn't react. About a week went by and still Hickok's gold watch was in Tutt's possession. The goading and mocking continued at every opportunity, eventually coming to a head in what was a set-up by Tutt and his associates. A group of them wandered into the Lyon House Hotel and told Hickok that Tutt would be wearing his beloved watch the following morning in the town square. If he was trying to draw Hickok into a gunfight, Tutt was taking a massive risk; he must have known that his chances of winning were remote. Hickok was as a good a shot with a gun as he was a poker player.

The next day just before 10 am, Tutt duly walked across the town square, openly wearing a gold pocket watch, clearly visible hanging from his waist pocket. On hearing of Tutt's presence, Hickok made his way to the square to begin discussing terms for the return of the pocket watch. It didn't start well because Tutt was now demanding $45, but Hickok was adamant that he only owed $25. Although there was a stalemate over how much money should be paid, both men kept calm and they ended up going to the Lyon House Hotel to have a drink, but once again nothing was resolved and Tutt left with Hickok's watch still hanging from his waist pocket. A short while later he returned to the town square, still wearing the watch.

At just before 6 pm that same evening, Hickok walked slowly towards the square, his Colt Navy revolver in his right hand. As soon as townsfolk saw him walking along holding his gun they quickly scattered for cover. Before long Tutt appeared walking from the opposite direction. They were about 75ft apart when Hickok stopped and called out, 'Dave, here I am,' before cocking his pistol and holstering it. 'Don't you come across here with that watch.' There was no reply. Tutt simply stood with his hand on his pistol.

Both men took up a sideways duelling position. Tutt reached for his pistol, Hickok followed suit and after drawing his pistol steadied it by resting it on his opposite forearm, quickly taking aim at Tutt. Both men fired almost simultaneously. Tutt's round missed whilst Hickok's bullet struck Tutt in his left side, between the fifth and seventh ribs. He didn't die instantly, initially running on to the porch of the town's courthouse before returning to the square, where he called out 'Boys I'm killed' then collapsed and died.

Tutt's death was certainly of his own doing, as he created the entire situation. He must have realised that Hickok wasn't going to let the issue about his beloved gold pocket watch just go away; he couldn't ignore him even if he wanted to. Tutt had openly embarrassed him in front of a packed saloon and would have known that if it came to a gunfight between him and Hickok, he was a strong contender to come off worst.

It appears that his plan was to goad Hickok into drawing on him, which would have given Tutt's associates the excuse to gun him down, but he never took the bait. In the end, Tutt had no option but to go through with the gunfight; if he didn't he would have looked like a coward, and his own credibility would have been in tatters.

As appeared to be the norm in such cases, the next day a warrant was issued for the arrest of Wild Bill Hickok. After his arrest, bail was initially refused – normal procedure in such cases – but Hickok managed to persuade the magistrate that he wouldn't 'leave town' and posted a substantial bail of $2,000. Later the same day, the charge against Hickok was amended from one of murder to the lesser charge of manslaughter.

The eagerly awaited trial began on 3 August 1865, with Hickok being represented by the former Union military governor of Arkansas, Colonel John S. Phelps.

At the outbreak of the American Civil War, Phelps returned to his home town of Springfield and enlisted in the Union Army, not as an officer but a private in Captain Coleman's Company of Missouri Infantry.

Following the Union defeat on 19 August 1861, at the Battle of Wilson's Creek just outside Springfield, where they sustained some 1,300 casualties, Phelps and the remainder of his colleagues retreated to the nearby town of Rolla. This was his first experience of fighting during the war.

But his time in the lower ranks was a short-lived experience, because on 2 October 1861, he was promoted to lieutenant colonel, and just ten weeks later on 19 December 1861, he was further promoted when he became a colonel. Phelps, having been given special permission by President Abraham Lincoln to raise his own regiment, did so and named it Phelps Regiment, Missouri Volunteer Infantry. In March 1862, having spent the winter garrisoned at Fort Wyman in Rolla, Phelps and his men were involved in some fierce fighting at Pea Ridge in Arkansas, which took place over the two days of 7 and 8 March 1862. The fighting resulted in a Union victory, with the defeat meaning the Confederates never seriously threatened the state of Missouri for the rest of the war.

On 13 May 1862, Phelps was mustered (received honourable discharge) which meant that for him the war, or at least the fighting, was over. Shortly afterwards, in July 1862, he was appointed as the military governor of Arkansas by President Abraham Lincoln. It wasn't a position he held for long, having to resign due to ill health.

The judge at Hickok's manslaughter trial was the eloquently named Sempronius H. Boyd, and the prosecution case was led by Major Robert Washington Fyan, who had also served in the Union Army during the American Civil War.

Hickok's plea was one of self-defence, which was rather strange, as technically, under state law, and in this particular case, such a claim had no validity as Hickok had gone to the square armed, looking for Tutt and expecting a fight. He most certainly hadn't taken all reasonable steps to avoid it. Why Phelps hadn't advised his client on this point is unclear.

Even though there were some twenty-five witnesses in the square at the time of the gunfight, only four of them admitted having watched it. Of these, two said that both Hickok and Tutt fired, but neither could say who fired first. One of them had been standing immediately behind Hickok (which seems a dangerous place to have been), so he only saw Hickok draw, but didn't know if that had been before or after Tutt had opened fire. Another witness said that he hadn't seen or heard Tutt discharge his weapon, but agreed that he had noticed that his pistol had discharged one cartridge. Everyone else who had been in the square at the time of the shooting claimed that they hadn't actually seen the fight, but had heard only one shot being fired. This last claim seems somewhat strange, because of Hickok's rather unusual style of drawing his weapon, resting it on his other arm, taking aim, then firing. This would have provided an opponent every opportunity to fire, possibly even more than once.

After having listened to all available evidence the jury determined that Hickok had been justified in shooting Tutt, as it was the latter who had directly instigated the matter by stealing Hickok's watch, and was the first to overtly show aggression.

As two of the witnesses had stated that Tutt had drawn first, the jury deemed that Hickok was justified in his claim of self-defence – despite what the law said to the contrary – and that Hickok's shooting of Tutt was legal.

The other aspect which went in Hickok's favour was the fact that from the moment Tutt had taken his watch, he had showed great restraint and presented Tutt with numerous opportunities to do the right thing and return the watch. It certainly was unusual for a man to be so openly disrespected so many times and not react in a violent or an aggressive manner. In this case, Hickok was disrespected in two different ways. Firstly, by the original theft of his watch, and secondly when Tutt took to openly wearing it around town.

At the end of the case, Judge Boyd provided the jury with some direction, which it has to be said was both confusing and contradictory. He started by informing them that their only option in law was to find the defendant guilty, but then added that if they so chose, they could apply the unwritten law option of the 'fair fight' and acquit the defendant, an action known as jury nullification. This generally occurs when members of a jury in a criminal trial find a defendant is guilty of the offence they have been charged with, but choose to acquit the defendant because the jurors also believe that the law itself is either unjust, that the prosecutor has misapplied the law in the defendant's case, or that the potential punishment for breaking the law is too harsh. In essence it allowed a jury to make a decision contrary to what the law said they could.

On 6 August 1865, having listened to the judge's advice and deliberated for less than two hours, the jury decided to acquit Hickok. He was a free man with his credibility still intact, although not everybody was happy about the outcome, including a well-known Springfield lawyer who gave a speech from the courthouse steps after the verdict had been announced about how wrong the decision was. But putting his negativity about the outcome to one side, the result was widely expected and regarded as being justifiable provocation for Hickok to resort to turning to his Navy Colt pistol to resolve the matter once and for all.

Davis Tutt's body was initially buried in the Springfield City Cemetery, but some eighteen years later, in March 1883, it was disinterred and reburied in Maple Park Cemetery, by his half-brother Lewis Tutt, a former slave who was the son of Tutt's father and one of his slaves.

Some weeks after the end of the trial, Hickok was interviewed for *Harper's Magazine* by Colonel George Ward Nichols. It was an interview that would eventually turn an unknown gunfighter into one of the great legends of the Wild West. The finished article appeared in *Harper's Magazine* and went under the simple and to the point heading of *Wild Bill*. His immortalisation by Nichols' article drew criticism from a number of Kansas newspapers, who felt it exaggerated Hickok's exploits.

Gunslingers

Life was certainly harsh in the old American Wild West, where as well as lawmen most towns had a sheriff and deputy. There were also deputy US marshals, who had been created by the Judiciary Act of 1789.

It wasn't an easy existence. If men disagreed with each other or felt wronged in some way, many used their hand guns to settle the argument.

Although the term gunslinger is a relatively new invention, coined in an attempt to glamorise that period of American history as portrayed in films and books, it is an apt word to describe some of the men who lived their lives by toting their weapons.

On **5 April 1879**, a gunfight took place in the Long Branch Saloon, in Dodge City, Kansas between Frank Loving and Levi Richardson, both regular gamblers at the saloon.

Frank Loving was just a 19-year-old youth who had been in Dodge City for less than a year, having moved there from Texas. He appears to have moved to the city with no other desire than to become a gambler. He certainly didn't aspire to become anything too taxing, but having said that, he wasn't stupid. He became friendly with the owner of the Long Branch Saloon, Chalkey Beeson, and through his lifestyle of gambling and frequenting saloons, he became acquainted with a number of notable gunmen, gamblers and lawmen of the day, including John Allen, Levi Richardson, Wyatt Earp, 'Doc' Holliday and Bat Masterson.

Levi Richardson was a man's man, as tough as they came and with a look on his face which didn't encourage unwanted conversation or loose words. Added to this was a reputation for being a hardened gunslinger, although nobody really knew who he had been in any gunfights with. Whatever the truth was it certainly hadn't done his reputation any harm at all.

The trouble between Richardson and Loving began in early 1879, when the pair argued over Loving's claims that Richardson had been making advances to his young wife, Mattie Loving. To begin with the dispute was little more than taunts and verbal confrontation, which amounted to nothing too dramatic. This behaviour between the pair carried on for a couple of months, but then in March 1879 they became involved in a fight where punches were thrown, and as they parted Richardson told Loving that he would blow his guts out and called him a cocky son of a bitch. But nothing further happened as Loving wasn't armed; he simply turned and walked away.

Such circumstances were seldom just forgotten about; pride, respect and reputation saw to that. They usually festered and one night after a few too many drinks, the issue once again raised its head. This is exactly what happened in this case. On 5 April 1879, Richardson went looking for Loving at the Long Branch Saloon, but he wasn't there. Instead of leaving, Richardson joined in a game of poker in which he became quite engrossed. Loving finally arrived in the saloon at about 9 pm. He noticed Richardson playing poker, but went and sat down at the bar and ordered a drink. After a while, Richardson joined Loving at the bar and the two men began to talk. To start with everything appeared to be quite calm until, without warning, Richardson shouted out, 'You wouldn't fight anything you damned son of a bitch.' On this occasion Loving was armed and calmly replied, 'Try me and see.' Without replying Richardson drew his gun, and a split second later Loving did the same. Both men began blasting away at each other just a few feet apart. In a matter of just a few seconds eleven shots had been fired and once the smoke had dispersed, the two men were still both standing. Loving, who had five shots fired at him, suffered nothing more damaging than a graze on the hand. Richardson on the other hand had been shot in the chest, the side and one of his arms. Having heard the shots the town's marshal, Charlie Basset and deputy marshal Duffey, quickly made their way to the saloon, Duffey arriving first to find Richardson was still on his feet, taking hold of him just before he fell to the floor dead.

As was the norm in such matters, Loving was arrested and taken to the town's jail. A coroner's inquest took place two days later, where it was ruled that Loving had opened fire in self-defence and he left the court a free man without a blemish to his name. It is remarkable that Richardson managed to miss Loving with each of the five shots that he fired, especially since there were just feet and inches between them. At that distance a man doesn't even have to take aim. All he does is stretch his arm out, point his gun in the direction of the man he is about to fight, and pull the trigger. Even allowing for the stress and trauma of the moment, at such a close distance it is extremely difficult to miss,

How far Richardson's liking for Loving's wife had gone, was never revealed.

On **22 January 1880**, a gunfight took place at the Close and Patterson's Variety Hall in Las Vegas, New Mexico. But this was no ordinary gunfight.

The Dodge City Gang, which was a group of Kansas gunfighters and gamblers, had moved into Las Vegas, New Mexico in 1879, where they dominated the local economy and politics. As with many boomtowns of the American Wild West, they attracted a plethora of different types of people. Some were good and some weren't so good, but there was always a combination of cowboys, opportunists, gamblers and outlaws. Sometimes one man met all four criteria.

The Dodge City Gang consisted of gunmen such as John Joshua Webb, 'Arkansas' Dave Rudabaugh, and Dave Mather, with an associate of theirs being 'Doc' Holliday. The man who ran the show was Hyman G. Niell, better known as Hoodoo Brown, who had managed to wangle his way into becoming the local justice of the peace. Holding such a position allowed him and his men to control all of the gambling houses in Las Vegas, which meant raking in large profits, whilst still having a public face of legitimacy. It also meant that it was nigh on impossible for anybody else to try and muscle in on their 'business'.

One of the gang, Dave Mather, had a reputation for being a gun for hire, but as was the case with many a gunman of the American Wild West, there wasn't too much in the way of documented proof about his so-called exploits with a gun. It appears that all a man needed to prove his credentials as a gunslinger were myths and embellished stories of his fighting prowess.

On 22 January 1880, the town's marshal Joe Carson and Mather went to the Close and Patterson's Variety Hall after receiving complaints from citizens of a number of rowdy customers inside. Whether Mather had actually been deputised at the time has never been officially confirmed, but I believe that he was for two reasons. Why else would he have been in company with Joe Carson, and secondly because at the time Las Vegas had a restriction on the carrying of guns within the confines of the town's limits, and Mather was overtly armed for everybody to see. With such an order in effect, even though Mather was a part of the Dodge City Gang, he wouldn't have been allowed to carry a firearm if he wasn't a deputy, because it would have made it difficult to enforce a restriction on the carrying of guns on others coming into town.

On arriving at the Variety Hall, Marshal Carson and Mather were confronted by four drunken and rowdy cowboys, who were hell-bent on having a good time. They were T. J. House, James West, John Dorsey and William 'Big' Randall. Without any delay, Marshal Carson informed the men that they had to hand over their firearms because of the town's restrictions that were in place, but all of the men refused. Nobody knows who drew first or who fired first, but a gunfight quickly ensued. Marshal Carson was killed almost immediately with one of the first shots fired. The talking was long over with and Mather opened up, firing at lightning speed, and in no time at all he had killed Randall and wounded West and Dorsey, with the latter managing to escape with T. J. House.

The two men were captured just two weeks later and brought back to the Las Vegas jail to join the wounded West to await a trial, but before they could be put before the courts, an angry mob of local men broke into the San Miguel County jail, dragged the three men outside and hanged them. It is strange to think that such an event could occur when taking into account the hold and control the Dodge City Gang had over the town, especially as it was Mather who was on duty at the time. Some of the townspeople were starting to question how it could have happened when Mather had happily stood up to the four men at the Variety Hall. Not a single bullet had been fired to try and defend the three men who were in custody, which strongly suggests that Mather, or anyone else for that matter was at the jail. Such a situation doesn't seem in keeping with what would be expected.

But it was Mather's actions during the confrontation at the Variety Hall which would go on to make him a name to be remembered within the history of America's Wild West.

Below is a potted history of Mather's actions in the days after the Variety Hall shootings, as it will help provide a more complete history of the man and show just how dangerous he actually was.

Just three days after the gunfight at the Close and Patterson's Variety Hall, Mather, now the town's acting marshal, was called to deal with an incident between Joseph Castello and his bosses. During what had become a heated argument, Castello had drawn his pistol. When Mather arrived at the scene, Castello told him not to come any closer or he would open fire. Without saying a word, Mather drew his own pistol and fired a single shot, killing Castello before he even had time to fire his gun. The subsequent coroner's inquest saw the jury decide that Mather's shooting of Castello was justifiable and in self-defence.

In March 1880, the town of Las Vegas experienced two murders in the same day, both men having been shot. With no one allowed within the town's limits with any firearms other than the town's marshal and his deputies, the townsfolk didn't look too far for potential suspects. Mather resigned on 3 March 1880, although he didn't leave town until at least a couple of weeks later.

The next few years of Mather's life were somewhat at odds with his previous existence. He got into trouble with the law, but not as one might expect for killing a man in a gunfight, but for stealing a woman's dress, and counterfeiting; both offences saw him spend a number of months in prison. He was also charged with the theft of two diamond rings and a watch, charges which he was acquitted of on 13 April 1882.

Despite his criminality and his time spent in prison, Mather was hired as an assistant city marshal in Dodge City on 1 June 1883, but it was a job that he only did for nine months, before being replaced by Tom Nixon on 10 April 1884. This didn't go down well with Mather at all. His dismissal had come about because the city council passed a law making dance halls illegal within Dodge City. This was enforced against the Opera House saloon, which was owned by Mather, preventing him from operating as a dance hall. This in itself wasn't the real problem for Mather. What had annoyed him was that the Lady Gay Saloon, which also operated a dance hall, hadn't been banned from doing so. That and the fact that it was owned by none other than Tom Nixon.

This unfairness began a feud between the two men. Mather retaliated, not with violence or a gun, but by halving the price of his beer to just 5 cents a glass. But just as Mather hadn't taken the slight against himself lying down, neither did Nixon or the other Dodge City saloon bar owners. They put pressure on the company who supplied the beer to all of the saloons throughout Dodge City to stop supplying beer to Mather's Opera House saloon. The beer company complied.

The feud resulted in a gunfight between the two men on 18 July 1884, in which Mather was shot and wounded. But the matter didn't end there. Just three days later and with Mather still recovering from his wounds, the two men saw each other in Dodge City and an argument ensued between them. This time it was Mather who had the upper hand: he shot and killed Nixon.

A preliminary hearing took place, as was the norm in such matters, to determine whether the case should be sent to trial or thrown out and ruled to be self-defence. Despite the sheriff of Dodge City, Patrick Shugrue and the creditable Bat Masterson providing Mather with supporting testimony, the matter was sent for trial, but Mather's lawyer managed to get the trial dealt with at the court in Ford County. The trial began on 29 December 1884 and lasted only three days. It took the jury just seven minutes of deliberations before they announced their verdict to the court. They had found Mather not guilty.

As might be expected the case drew much attention from the Press. By way of example, the *Kinsley Mercury* wrote, 'the verdict was a proper one, as the weight of the testimony showed that Nixon was the aggressor in the affray and that Mather was justified in the shooting.' The *Dodge City Times* explained how 'the reading of the verdict, by the foreman of the jury, was interrupted by demonstrations of approval from the audience.'

If the articles in the Press were anything to go by, Mather's acquittal was a popular decision.

El Paso, Texas was the next port of call for a tale of a gunfight in the rugged times of the Wild West. On **14 April 1881**, in El Paso Street, El Paso, the confrontation which history has chosen to refer to as the 'Four Dead in Five Seconds Gunfight' took place.

Here is a brief outline of the background leading up to the fight.

On 14 April 1881, a large number of heavily armed Mexicans, believed to have been more than seventy-five, arrived in El Paso. They were looking for two of their vaqueros, or cowboys, who had gone missing whilst searching for some of their cattle that had been stolen in Mexico. The first problem this caused was having armed men in the town, as there was a no firearms within the city limits order in place in El Paso. If the authorities tried to impose this rule on the Mexicans and they didn't wish to comply, there was absolutely no way of being able to enforce it. The mayor of El Paso, Solomon Schutz, resolved the issue by making an exception for the Mexicans, and allowing them to hold on to their firearms.

Later the same day, an El Paso county constable, Gus Krempkau, led a posse out to a ranch some 13 miles outside of El Paso in the Upper Valley. It was owned by a man named Johnny Hale, who was also suspected of cattle rustling. After a search of the area near Hale's ranch, two bodies were recovered and taken back to El Paso. They were identified as being those of the two missing Mexicans.

A couple of days after the bodies of the two men had been brought back to El Paso, an inquest was held into their deaths. Constable Krempkau, a fluent Spanish speaker, acted as an interpreter in court. The outcome of the inquest was a finding that the American cattle rustlers, amongst which they included the ranch owner Hale, had discovered the two Mexicans, Sanchez and Juarique, and feared they would find their stolen cattle, and then return with a large number of their heavily armed colleagues to recover them. Two of the men who worked for Hale, Pervey and Fredericks, were accused of having carried out the murders of the two Mexicans, having been overheard bragging about killing two cowboys when they discovered them trailing their herd back to Hale's ranch during the evening of 13 and 14 April 1881.

There were a lot of people in El Paso, including the heavily armed Mexicans, and tensions were running high between them and the Americans, including John Hale and a friend of his, George Campbell, who had previously been the town marshal of El Paso. By the end of the inquest, Pervey and Fredericks were formally charged with the murders of the Mexicans Sanchez and Juarique, and immediately arrested. These actions appeased the Mexicans, who were happy that justice had been done, and they left El Paso to return to Mexico with the bodies of their compatriots so that they could receive a proper burial.

Marshal Dallas Stoudenmire, a noted gunfighter who had only become the marshal of El Paso on 11 April 1881, was one of those present at the inquest. Once the proceedings had come to an end, he left the courthouse and made his way across the street to have his dinner. At the same time, Constable Krempkau went to the saloon next door to retrieve his pistol and rifle, where he became embroiled in a disagreement with George Campbell concerning remarks he made about his courtroom translations, and the fact that he appeared extremely friendly with the Mexicans. A heavily intoxicated John Hale was also present, and also annoyed with Krempkau's involvement in the case, believing he had sided with the Mexicans against the Americans. Hale, who had been unarmed, suddenly grabbed one of Campbell's guns, shouting, 'George, I've got you covered,' before shooting Krempkau, who was sent sprawling against one of the saloon's front doors.

Marshal Stoudenmire, having heard the shot, jumped up from his dining chair at the Globe Restaurant, pulled out his pistols, and ran out into the street. While running, Stoudenmire fired wildly, which was extremely unusual for him, especially as he didn't know what had happened or who was involved. One of his loose rounds killed an innocent Mexican bystander by the name of Ochoa, who was simply running for cover. On hearing Stoudenmire's first shot, John Hale sobered up quickly and hid behind a thick pillar which afforded him an element of cover. But when he peered out from behind the pillar, Stoudenmire fired again, striking Hale right between the eyes, killing him instantly.

Campbell stepped from cover with his pistol drawn, saw Hale lying dead, and called out to Stoudenmire that this wasn't his fight. In the meantime Constable Krempkau, who hadn't been killed by the round Hale fired at him, but mistakenly believing that Campbell had shot him, then fired his pistol twice at Campbell before losing consciousness from loss of blood. Krempkau's first bullet struck Campbell's gun and broke his right wrist, while the second hit him in the foot. Campbell screamed in pain and scooped up his gun from the ground with his left hand. He should have left it well alone as this simply provided Stoudenmire with the opportunity to open fire, which he did. He whirled away from Hale and immediately fired at Campbell, hitting him in the stomach and causing him to drop his pistol for a second time, before collapsing to the ground. Stoudenmire walked slowly toward Campbell who no longer posed a threat. He glared at him and said nothing. Both Campbell and Krempkau died a matter of minutes later.

Witnesses to the shootings generally agreed that the incident lasted no more than five seconds after the first gunshot had been fired, although there were some who said it was more like ten seconds. Three of the four fatalities had been accounted for by Marshal Dallas Stoudenmire, with his twin .44 calibre Smith & Wesson revolvers.

Three Texas Rangers, who had been in El Paso and witnessed the incident, didn't intervene as they felt Stoudenmire had the situation well under control on his own.

What always amazes me about the Wild West, was nobody would ever let anything go, regardless of whether it was fair or unfair. Everybody wanted revenge, regardless of the circumstances. This incident was no different. Three days after the shootings of Hale and Campbell, James Manning, who had been a friend of the two dead men, arranged for a man by the name of Bill Johnson to kill Stoudenmire. The two men knew each other as Johnson had been a former deputy.

On the evening of 17 April 1881, whilst Stoudenmire was doing his last walk round of the day, an intoxicated Johnson was waiting for his chance to kill Stoudenmire. Whilst hiding up along the route he knew the marshal would take, his legs gave way, and he fell backwards, and in doing so discharged both barrels of the shotgun he was holding, narrowly missing Stoudenmire, who immediately opened fire with a volley of eight shots, two of which shot off Johnson's testicles, causing him to quickly bleed to death in excruciating pain.

One of the most famous gunfights of the Wild West era wasn't one man against another, but four against four. The background of why the gunfight actually took place, is as follows.

In an effort to reduce crime in Tombstone, much of which was gun related, the city council issued an order that restricted hand guns and rifles from being carried within the town's limits. All weapons had to be handed in at either the saloon or the livery. But not all cowboys who came into town for a few beers and the company of a woman appreciated being told that they had to hand over their guns. In fact, some outright refused to comply with the instruction. That was when the problems began and the town's lawmen earned their money.

On Wednesday, 26 October 1881, City Marshal Virgil Earp was told by some of Tombstone's concerned citizens that there were a number of cowboys in town who were carrying their guns and refusing to hand them in. These same men had been threatening the Earp brothers, Virgil, Wyatt and Morgan, for many months, because as lawmen they were starting to have an impact on their criminal activities. This was one of those situations that regardless of how the Earp brothers felt, they simply couldn't back down because if they did, they knew that they would be handing the town over to a bunch of lawless, murdering cowboys, who didn't much care for anything or anybody, other than themselves. On being informed of the violation, Virgil, deputy Morgan Earp, along with temporary deputies, Wyatt Earp and John 'Doc' Holliday, went looking for the five men concerned in an effort to get the men to hand over their guns. The men in question were brothers Frank and Tom McLaury, Ike and Billy Clanton along with Billy Claiborne.

It was just before 3 pm on that fateful day that the Earps and Doc Holliday headed towards the town's Fremont Street, where they had been informed that the men they were looking for could be found. They finally found them at the town's OK Corral, which was quite a narrow location, squeezed in amongst three surrounding properties. As the nine men faced off against each other, Billy Claiborne and Ike Clanton had a last minute change of heart and decided a gunfight wasn't for them after all and ran off. By now the remaining seven men were standing no more than 10ft away from each other, possibly even closer.

Despite the best attempts by Virgil Earp to get the men to hand over their guns, they were having none of it, and refused to comply with the lawmen's request. Virgil shouted at the men to, 'throw up your hands, I want your guns'. With neither side backing down, there was always only going to be one outcome, and almost immediately the shooting started. It isn't exactly clear which side opened fire first.

By the time the gunfight was over, the McLaury brothers, Tom and Frank, and Billy Clanton were all dead. As for the 'good guys', Morgan Earp was shot and wounded by a round that cut across his back hitting both shoulder blades and a vertebra in his spine, but thankfully for Morgan it was a 'nick' or a graze. Virgil was shot through the calf of his right leg, and Doc Holliday sustained a flesh wound.

For the time of year it was an exceptionally cold and windy day in Tombstone. The weather added to the atmosphere of the occasion. Virgil Earp had even taken to wearing a long overcoat, not just to keep the cold out but also to hide the fact that he was carrying a short-barrelled shot gun.

On Sunday, 30 October 1881, Ike Clanton, one of the two men who had run off before the gunfight started, filed murder charges against the three Earp brothers and Doc Holliday. Despite what had happened, the allegation was taken seriously. So seriously in fact that on Monday, 31 October 1881, a preliminary hearing was convened by Justice Wells Spicer to determine if there was sufficient evidence for the matter to be sent for trial.

Judge Spicer took both written and oral testimony from approximately thirty witnesses, which made the trial somewhat drawn out and more than a month in duration. In evidence that was quite damning for the Earps and Doc Holliday, Sheriff Behan stated that the McLaury brothers and Billy Clanton hadn't only shown no resistance whatsoever, but they weren't even armed. Behan, who was obviously no friend of his fellow lawmen, continued with his evidence by saying that Tom McLaury actually threw open his coat to show that he wasn't armed and that the first two shots that were fired came from Doc Holliday, who, he said, was using a nickel-plated revolver. Another witness gave a slightly different version to Sheriff Behan. He said that the only weapon he saw Doc Holliday with, was a 'Messenger' shotgun, just before the gunfight started, and he certainly made no mention of a nickel-plated revolver.

The prosecution had certainly approached the case in a professional and detailed manner. Their evidence from witnesses, regardless of whether it was true or fabricated, was considerable. They had gone all out in an effort to persuade Judge Spicer that there was sufficient evidence for the matter to be sent for a full trial.

On the second day of the hearings, William Allen testified for the prosecution that the firing was started by the Earps and Doc Holliday. 'I think it was Doc Holliday who fired first,' he said. Sheriff Johnny Behan gave evidence that he had tried to prevent the confrontation. 'I told them I was down there for the purpose of disarming the Clantons and McLaurys. They wouldn't heed me, paid no attention. And I said, "Gentlemen, I am Sheriff of this County, and I am not going to allow any trouble if I can help it." They brushed past me.'

Defending the Earps and Doc Holliday was experienced trial lawyer, Thomas Fitch, who began with an opening speech which included a detailed history of previous problems that the Earps, in their capacity as lawmen, had already experienced with the Clantons and the McLaurys. He then went on to tell the court that Wyatt Earp's only intention right from the outset was to disarm the five cowboys, and that he, his brothers and Doc Holliday only fired in self-defence.

Witnesses who had been produced by the prosecution were cross-examined by Fitch, who managed to illicit either contradictory accounts from what they had previously given, or they suddenly could no longer remember what they actually saw.

After hearing all the witnesses' testimonies, Judge Spicer ruled on 30 November 1881, that there wasn't enough evidence to indict any of the Earp brothers or Doc Holliday. In his opinion the evidence indicated that the four men acted within the law and that Doc Holliday and Wyatt Earp had both been deputised by Virgil Earp, prior to the shoot-out.

The Earp brothers and Doc Holliday were free men, but the not-so-law-abiding cowboys of Tombstone were far from happy about the outcome of the hearing, fully expecting that they would have been sent to trial. This wasn't something they were just going to walk away from, they were bitter and angry men, especially Ike Clanton.

Despite the fact that it was only a preliminary hearing, both the defence and the prosecution teams presented their complete case as if it was a full trial. But there was a reason for this.

As far as the prosecution was concerned, it was important that they made a sufficiently strong enough case with plenty of evidence, because historically criminal charges were usually dismissed if the prosecution failed to do so. As for the defence, it was a slightly different matter, but just as important. The Earps and Doc Holliday's defence lawyer, Tom Fitch, was very shrewd. He knew full well that Judge Spicer was a Republican, and like the Earps he had no time for the lawless element of society. It was therefore imperative for Fitch to have a strong enough case to convince Spicer to rule that there was insufficient evidence to send it to trial. If he failed, he knew that his clients were in real danger of being found guilty. Fitch would have worked out that if the case was sent to trial, his clients would more than likely face a pro-Democrat jury, but one that was also pro-cowboy as well.

For both sides there was always an issue concerning witnesses. Frontier life was transient to say the least. People came and went on a regular basis. Some conveniently forgot what they had actually seen once they realised what a potentially dangerous situation they were in, and others were actually killed, the result of some drunken bar-room brawl.

It has to be said that the Earps' and Holliday's case was greatly helped by their decision to employ Tom Fitch. He was without doubt excellent at his job and a real firebrand in the courtroom. His power of observation and recollection was simply outstanding. His ability to get prosecution witnesses to provide conflicting evidence during cross-examination was incredible and undoubtedly helped in discrediting much of the evidence they had initially provided so convincingly. There were several occasions when he obtained testimony from prosecution witnesses, only to then compare it with statements that were corroborated by other witnesses that conflicted with the prosecution witnesses' original testimony.

It seems quite clear that many of the prosecution witnesses had lied, or been economical with the truth when giving their evidence. In response to questions by Fitch, there were many occasions when these witnesses could only respond with, 'I don't remember', which was hardly convincing testimony. Such responses were more helpful to the defence than they were the prosecution.

The prosecution team was quite interesting. The chief prosecutor was Lyttleton Price, who was well-known locally as a staunch supporter of the Republican Party. His assistant was Ben Goodrich. The third man on the team was Will McLaury, whose usual place of practising law was Texas. He was also the brother of Frank and Tom McLaury, two of the men killed by the Earps and Doc Holliday, so he was most definitely keen to have them found guilty and had come to Tombstone just to be involved in the case.

Regardless of who and how many people were part of the prosecution team, they were no match for Fitch and his courtroom skills. An example of this was his cross-examination of the Cochise County sheriff, Johnny Bevan, who had testified that he had seen Doc Holliday holding a shotgun before the gunfight started, but then went on to claim he had seen him subsequently firing a nickel-plated pistol. It is unlikely that he had one weapon with him on his way to the OK Corral, but changed it once he had arrived.

When it comes to giving evidence in court, the credibility of the witness is all important, especially if they are an upstanding member of the community or hold a position of rank, trust or influence. Sheriff Johnny Behan certainly held a position of rank and influence. He had testified that he didn't tell Virgil on the night of the gunfight that he had acted properly. Certain and compelling evidence from a sheriff; well at least it was until it was contradicted by another witness who just happened to be a deputy district attorney. The man in question, Winfield Scott Williams, who was with the sheriff and Virgil Earp when that conversation took place, gave testimony that Sheriff Behan had in fact told Virgil Earp that one of the McLaury brothers had been the first man to drawn his gun, and that he had said, 'you did perfectly right'.

Despite Behan refuting Williams' version of the conversation, the damage had already been done, because regardless of which of the two men was telling the truth, the words of a deputy district attorney had more credibility than those of a county sheriff. All Fitch needed to do was to place sufficient doubt in Judge Spicer's mind for him to dismiss the case against his clients.

Fitch didn't stop there. He wasn't taking any chances when it came to the outcome he wanted to achieve for his clients. He then went after Ike Clanton and was able to throw doubt over his credibility about a conversation he had with Wyatt Earp, concerning a reward offered by Wells Fargo for the capture of those who had robbed their coaches. This proved not to be the case. Ike Clanton also denied having had a conversation with Ned Boyle on the morning of the fatal gunfight; this was in direct contradiction to what Boyle had said.

Ike Clanton certainly didn't come across as a credible witness. Whilst being cross-examined by Fitch, Clanton used the phrase, 'I don't remember' a total of fourteen times. This, and the highlighted contradictions of other witnesses' testimony, totally discredited Clanton as a credible witness.

There were so many flaws with the prosecution's case, it was clear that their preparation for the hearing was just not up to the required standard necessary for the judge find in their favour. They had definitely not looked at nor considered the credibility or abilities of any of their witnesses to deal with the pressures of being cross-examined in court.

A good example of this is Ike Clanton, who had brought the case against the Earps and Doc Holliday. He had claimed that the Earps were out to murder him, yet once the gunfight began, Ike Clanton ran off, and there was no attempt by any of the Earps or Doc Holliday to shoot or to otherwise try and kill him.

The day after the gunfight at the OK Corral, a coroner's inquest was held into the events surrounding it. The jury were only told the known facts of the gunfight and weren't asked to pass comment on whether the shootings were lawful or criminal.

It was generally accepted that despite his personal views or politics, Judge Spicer dealt with the preliminary hearing in a fair and balanced manner. Having said that, he made two decisions which undoubtedly helped the Earps and Doc Holliday. Firstly he allowed Wyatt Earp to give his evidence from a pre-written statement. The issue here wasn't so much what Wyatt Earp had to say, rather the fact that by reading out a prepared statement, he wasn't allowed to be cross-examined in open court by the prosecution. Although it wasn't usual practice at the time, it was permitted by Section 133 of Arizona law which held that presenting a written statement meant the prosecution was prevented from then cross-examining a witness or defendant.

What was unclear, and open to interpretation, was whether a defendant could simply read from a written statement. In

Wyatt Earp's case, Judge Spicer certainly interpreted matters in his favour. When the prosecution objected, Spicer dismissed their motion, simply saying, 'the statute was very broad, he could make any statement he pleased, whether previously prepared or not'.

What was an even more amazing decision was when Spicer went to the home of witness Addie Borland, after she had delivered some confusing testimony in court. Spicer went as far as to get her to return to court, re-take the stand and answer his questions. She gave evidence to the effect that she didn't see the McLaurys or Billy Clanton raise their hands to surrender. This was in direct contradiction to what the prosecution witnesses, Wes Fuller, Billy Claiborne and Ike Clanton had claimed, although the latter of these two ran off before the gunfight began.

It was fair to say that the prosecution were far from happy with Spicer's conduct in relation to Addie Borland, and they told him so in no uncertain terms, but their protestations were to no avail.

Spicer's decision in the matter was announced on 30 November 1881. He was critical of Virgil Earp's decision to request the assistance of his brother Wyatt and their friend Doc Holliday, even though both of them had been made deputies by Virgil. Spicer went as far as to call it 'an injudicious and censurable act'. He added that although he believed Virgil's actions had been unwise, he couldn't attach any criminality to it.

Spicer provided an extremely long explanation of how and why he had arrived at his decision, which to some sounded more like an attempt at justifying it, than anything else. As for Ike Clanton, he wasn't happy with the outcome. He, more than most, found it hard to accept that not only had his brother been murdered, but that those responsible for his death had walked away scot-free. So keen was he for revenge that he tried once again to have the Earps and Doc Holliday charged with murder in the nearby silver mining town of Contention City, in Cochise, Arizona, but a grand jury there accepted Judge Spicer's ruling and refused Ike Clanton's application.

Remarkably, three days after the events at the OK Corral, rather than being congratulated for their sterling efforts that day, the Tombstone city council suspended Virgil Earp as a city marshal pending the outcome of the preliminary hearing. He was eventually exonerated of any wrong doing, but still his reputation suffered as a result, despite the fact that he, his brothers and Holliday were only doing their jobs.

The issue about whether Doc Holliday and Morgan Earp were actual lawmen at the time of the gunfight seems clouded, not as to whether they were, but because of the more likely outcome if Virgil Earp had either gone to the OK Corral on his own or just with his brother Wyatt. Both men, outnumbered and out-gunned, would have undoubtedly been killed, and history changed for ever more.

A tale of the Wild West that never went down in the annals of history with any great degree of importance, but which was widely reported at the time, took place on 21 August 1884, in Hunnewell, Kansas. The reason why history has largely forgotten this particular gunfight is because none of those who took part in it, were that well known, before or after the event.

Hunnewell was a prosperous cattle town, with the Leavenworth, Lawrence and Galveston Railroad providing quick access to the stockyards in Kansas City. It was popular with large numbers of cowboys who worked on the surrounding ranches and corrals, and to help cater for them it had a hotel, two general stores, a barber's shop, two dance halls and eight saloons. It was environment which catered for violence as a way of the men letting off steam and settling their differences. It is maybe somewhat surprising to learn that at the time the town had neither marshal, sheriff nor deputies to help uphold the peace or protect the townsfolk; incidents of crime or cattle rustling were usually dealt with by the ranchers themselves.

On 21 August 1884, two cowboys went to the town's *Hanley's Saloon*, got drunk and started causing problems. The two men were Oscar Halsell and Clem Barfoot. Two lawmen from Kansas, who were just passing through and in the saloon for a drink, attempted to calm the men down and bring an end to the situation. This quickly degenerated into an argument and the drawing of pistols by several of those present. There is no record of who drew and fired first, but when the gunfight that followed had finished, Barfoot was dead and Deputy Sheriff Ed Scotten lay mortally wounded. Nobody was ever prosecuted in relation to the death of Scotten.

Oscar Halsell went on to become a prosperous rancher who employed many notable gunmen of the day.

Commodore Stephen Decatur, United States Navy. Killed in a duel with Commodore James Barron on 22 March 1820.

Duel between American Vice President Aaron Burr and Alexander Hamilton on 11 July 1804. After the painting by J. Mund.

Vice President Aaron Burr (1804).

Alexander Peresvet fighting Chelubey, 8 September 1380, before the Battle of Kulikovo.

Anti-duelling pamphlet from 1804.

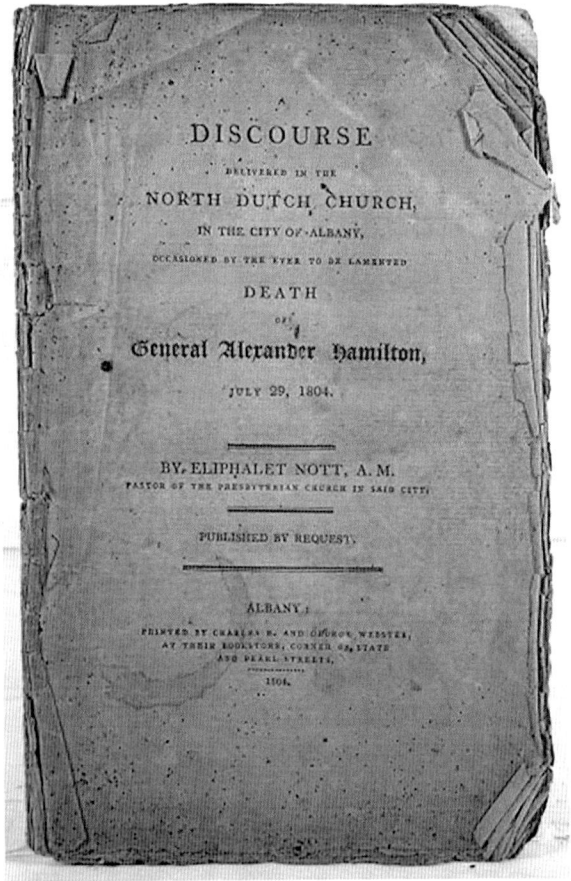

DISCOURSE

DELIVERED IN THE

NORTH DUTCH CHURCH,

IN THE CITY OF ALBANY,

OCCASIONED BY THE EVER TO BE LAMENTED

DEATH

OF

General Alexander Hamilton,

JULY 29, 1804.

BY ELIPHALET NOTT, A. M.

PASTOR OF THE PRESBYTERIAN CHURCH IN SAID CITY.

PUBLISHED BY REQUEST.

ALBANY:

PRINTED BY CHARLES R. AND GEORGE WEBSTER,
AT THEIR BOOKSTORE, CORNER OF STATE
AND PEARL STREETS.

1804.

Aulus Cornelius Cossus carries the head of the Etruscan King Lars Tolumnius during the Battle of Fidenae, 437BC.

Depiction of judicial combat from the Dresden code, mid-fourteenth century.

Robert the Bruce defeats de Bohun on the eve of the Battle of Bannockburn, 23 June 1314.

Plaque on the home of Commodore Stephen Decatur in Lafayette Square, Washington, United States.

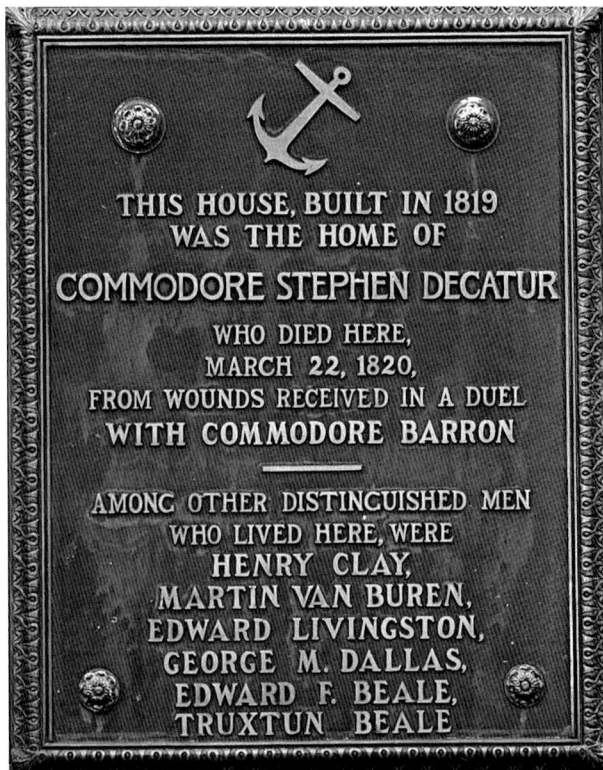

THIS HOUSE, BUILT IN 1819
WAS THE HOME OF
COMMODORE STEPHEN DECATUR
WHO DIED HERE,
MARCH 22, 1820,
FROM WOUNDS RECEIVED IN A DUEL
WITH COMMODORE BARRON

AMONG OTHER DISTINGUISHED MEN
WHO LIVED HERE, WERE
HENRY CLAY,
MARTIN VAN BUREN,
EDWARD LIVINGSTON,
GEORGE M. DALLAS,
EDWARD F. BEALE,
TRUXTUN BEALE

A depiction of a duel in the Bois de Boulogne, near Paris. The image appeared in *Harper's Weekly*, January 1875.

Depiction of the pistol duel between Alexander Pushkin and Georges-Charles D'Anthès, January 1837.

Depiction of a duel with swords, 1777.

Duel between Eugene Onegin and Vladimir Lensky in Alexander Pushkin's 1899 novel, *Onegin*.

A duel between French Prime Minister Charles Floquet and General Georges Boulanger, 1888.

A painting of a German duel, 1900.

A mosaic of
a duel between
Astyanax and
Kale, c.400BC.

A painting of gladiators resting after a fight in Ancient Roman times.

The Zliten mosaic depicting gladiators from around AD200.

A drawing of Wild Bill Hickok having just fought a duel in 1867.

A painting of Kenelm Digby
by Anthony van Dyck, 1630s.

Photograph of the 1967 duel between Monsieur René Ribière and Monsieur Gaston Defferre.

Preparing to compete in the duelling event at the 1908 Olympic Games.

Painting of the duel between Miyamoto Musashi and Sasaki Kojiro, 1612.

Duellist Otto von Bismarck, 1865.

Depiction of Pierre Bonaparte shooting Victor Noir, 1869.

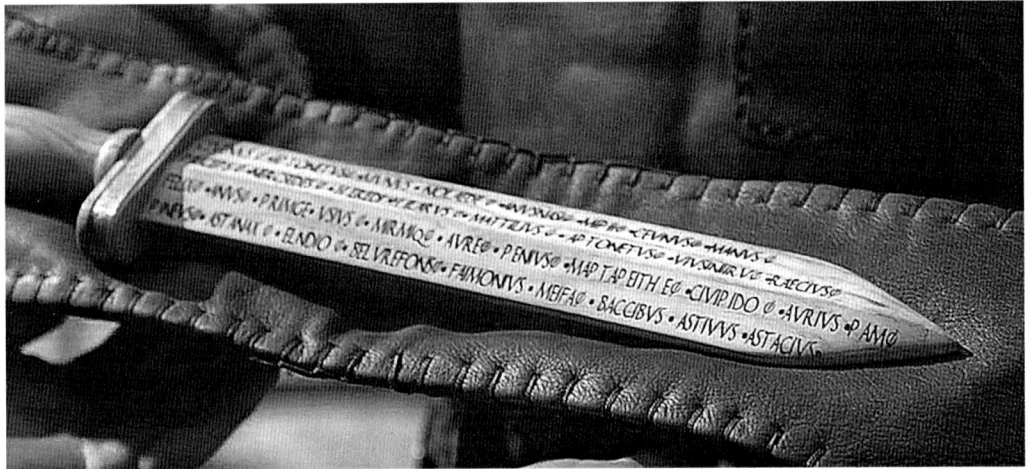

A Rudis sword from Ancient Roman times.

A painting of Japan's Sasaki Kojiro, c.1612.

A painting of the Challenge of Barletta, 1503.

An American town in the Wild West, c.1870.

The Petticoat Duelists.

A depiction of the Petticoat Duelists, Lady Almeria Braddock and Mrs Elphinstone, 1792.

Ben Salfield, who took part in the last known duel to have taken place in the UK in 1994.

CHAPTER SIX

Newspaper Articles of Duelling

An interesting and brief article about duelling appeared in the *Dublin Intelligence* on Saturday, 26 May 1711:

> The title of the Earl of Bath is extinct by the death of his Lordship, and the estate goes to 3 female heirs. By the act of passing against Duelling we hear the penalty of it is, that it incapacitates any one that does it, from having the benefit of the Laws of the Realm. The Coroner's inquest that sat on the body of Sir Chomley Dering, brought it in wilful murder, notwithstanding Sir Chomley forgave Mr Thornhill before he expired, and declared he was the cause of his own death.

The correct spelling of his name was in fact Cholmeley Dering and he was the 4th Baronet of Surrenden in Pluckley, Kent. He was elected as the MP for Kent in the 1705 general election, although he lost that seat in 1708. However, he was elected as the MP for Saltash, Cornwall, in a by-election on 7 December 1708. In the 1710 general election, because of the voting system at the time, he was elected to represent both Saltash and Kent, and he chose Kent.

On 7 May 1711, he was dining with friends at an inn near Hampton Court when he became involved in an argument with a man by the name of Richard Thornhill. What it was over or how it came to being, isn't recorded. It quickly degenerated into a brawl, with the men punching each other in the ensuing struggle, and before they could be separated by their associates, Dering kicked Thornhill so hard in the face that several of his teeth were knocked out.

Still incensed by what had happened, Thornhill sent Dering a note later that day challenging him to a duel at Tothill Fields in Westminster on the morning of 9 May 1711. Dering accepted the challenge and it was agreed that both men would use pistols. The two men went ahead with the duel, each firing one round. Thornhill fired first, striking Dering with what was to be a fatal wound. At one stage they were so close that their pistols were almost touching. Dering fired as he was falling to the ground, resulting in his shot spiralling harmlessly into the air. He died just a matter of minutes later.

Dering had married a merchant's daughter, Mary Fisher, on 17 July 1704, but tragically she died just three years later in 1707, when she was just 20 years of age. It is believed possibly whilst giving birth to their second child, Cholmeley.

Thornhill was tried for the crime of murder at the Old Bailey on 18 May 1711, but due to the original provocation by Dering, he was convicted of the lesser charge of manslaughter. An added twist to this duel was that they had started it with swords. I have not discovered what term of custodial sentence, if any, Thornhill was sentenced to, but what is known is that on 20 August 1711, he was murdered at Turnham Green public park in Chiswick, London, when he was attacked and stabbed by two men who made comments that suggested that their deed was to avenge Thornhill's shooting of Dering. Neither man was ever traced.

The *Ipswich Journal* dated Saturday, 26 June 1736, included the following article concerning the practice of duelling in France:

> Since the duel fought by the Grand Prior of France who grows better, but not out of danger, the practice of duelling is becoming so fashionable in Paris, that no less than eight of those battles have been fought there lately, and were attended with such fatality in each engagement. Death happened to be a certain lot of all but one of the combatants, but nothing is so singular as the contention which happened between a hot young Abbot, and another amorous spark, who both courted the favours of the amiable young lady, and happened to meet at once in her apartment. The spark unable to bear a rival drove at the Abbot with his fist, which so provoked the reverend gentleman, that he immediately ran for a sword, and without any ceremony fell to cut and slash his rival, and after an obstinate fight, killed him on the spot.

A very brief and unusual story was included in the *Derby Mercury* dated Thursday, 16 December 1736. The brief article had in turn had originated in the *St James's Evening Post* in Dublin of 11 December:

> This week a certain Baronet and a certain High Sheriff were put under Arrest, by order of the Government, to prevent their Duelling.

These three lines, hardly worth including in a newspaper, serve to demonstrate just how class-driven society was back in 1736. The government stepped in to prevent the two men from taking part in the duel, but the newspapers reporting the matter didn't name either man. Would that same mode of deterrent and anonymity have been so forthcoming if both had been commoners or men not so well established and connected in society? We cannot know.

The *Derby Mercury* of Friday, 5 September 1746 included an article on its front page in relation to duelling:

> We are informed, that in the next session of parliament a Bill will be brought into the House of Commons, in order to extinguish the bloody and dangerous practice of duelling, which prevails more here than in any other country of Europe, to the great scandal of our laws, religious and civil, to both of which it is equally repugnant. In time of war also, when the service of the public gives every man an opportunity of finalizing his courage and love for the society at once, such recounters are especially unpardonable; the loss of every brave man's life, in such a season, being a peculiar misfortune, and calling for the more than ordinary notice of the legislature, which can never want many arguments to excite them to repressing a humour diametrically opposite to all government whatever.

As can be seen from the above article, in September 1746, attempts were already being made to prevent the practice of duelling in England, but that certainly wasn't the case in

Ireland as can be seen by the following newspaper article that appeared in the *Ipswich Journal* some two years later on Saturday, 17 September 1748:

> The honour of duelling is at present carried so high in this kingdom, that last week at Dungannan, a journeyman Taylor challenged a journeyman wig maker to fight him with sword and pistol in a saw-pit. The seconds were a journeyman barber and a journeyman baker; but by the timely interposition of an old Chelsea out-pensioner, the effusion of blood was prevented by his threats upon the first aggressor.

An article appeared in the *Newcastle Courant* dated Saturday, 8 November 1746, about the parliament of Great Britain, looking at banning the practice of duelling:

> We hear that a Bill will be brought into Parliament at the approaching Sessions, for preventing the bloody an un-Christian practice of duelling, by rendering it punishable with death, to give, or send, or to be privy to the giving or sending a challenge, on any pretence whatsoever; and taking away the benefit of clergy, in case of sudden rencounters, or from such as shall presume to act, on any occasion, as seconds; and it is further said, that provision will be made for the due execution of this law, so that rank, relations, or other circumstances of influence, shall make no difference amongst offenders.

It is interesting to note that the above article relates to November 1746, yet the last recorded and known case of a fatal duel to take place in England was in 1852, more than 100 years later.

Even though there were attempts to eradicate the practice of duelling, they didn't prevent an Irish duelling code being drawn up in 1777. It contained a total of twenty-six points, or 'Commandments' as they were referred to. They are listed here to show just how complicated the etiquette for the practice of duelling was, and how ridiculous the entire issue around honour and respect for the aristocracy and gentlemen was, when it so quickly and readily turned to throwing down a challenge to a duel because of an assumed or actual slight. It was almost if men wanted to be challenged or to offer such a challenge so that they could prove how manly they were.

1. The first offence requires the first apology, though the retort may have been more offensive than the insult. Example: A tells B he is impertinent. B retorts that he lies; yet A must make the first apology, because he gave the first offence, and B may explain away the retort by subsequent apology.

2. But if the parties would rather fight on, then, after two shots each, but in no case before B may explain first and A apologise afterwards. N.B. The above rules apply to all cases of offences in retort not of a stronger class than the example.

3. If a doubt exists who gave the first offence, the decision rests with the seconds. If they will not decide or cannot agree, the matter must proceed to two shots, or to a hit if the challenger requires it.

4. When the lie direct is the first offence, the aggressor must either beg pardon in express terms, exchange two shots previous to apology, or three shots followed by

explanation, or fire on till a severe hit be received by one party or another.

5. As a blow is strictly prohibited under any circumstances among gentlemen, no verbal apology can be received for such an insult. The alternatives therefore are: The offender handing a cane to the injured party to be used on his back, at the same time begging pardon, firing on until one or both are disabled; or exchanging three shots and then asking pardon without the proffer of the cane. N.B. If swords are used, the parties engage until one is well blooded, disabled or disarmed, or until, receiving a wound and blood being drawn, the aggressor begs pardon. N.B. A disarm is considered the same as a disable; the disarmer may (strictly) break his adversary's sword; but if it be the challenger who is disarmed, it is considered ungenerous to do so. In case the challenged be disarmed, and refused to ask pardon, or atone, he must not be killed, as formerly, but the challenger may lay his own sword on the aggressor's shoulder, then break the aggressor's sword, and say, 'I spare your life!' The challenged can never revive that quarrel, the challenger may.

6. If A gives B the lie and B retorts by a blow, being the two greatest offences, no reconciliation can take place till after two discharges each or a severe hit, after which B may beg A's pardon for the blow, and then A may explain simply for the lie, because a blow is never allowable, and the offence of the lie, therefore merges in it. N.B. Challenges for undivulged causes may be conciliated on the ground after one shot. An explanation or the slightest hit should be sufficient in such cases, because no personal offence transpired.

7. But no apology can be received in any case after the parties have actually taken their ground, without exchange of shots.

8. In the above case no challenger is obliged to divulge his causes of challenge, if private, unless required so to do before their meeting.

9. All imputations of cheating at play, races, etc., are to be considered equivalent to a blow, but may be reconciled after one shot, on admitting their falsehood and begging pardon publicly.

10. Any insult to a lady under a gentleman's care or protection is to be considered as by one degree a greater offence than if given to the gentleman personally, and to be regarded accordingly.

11. Offences originating or accruing from the support of ladies' reputations are to be considered less unjustifiable than any others of the same class, and as admitting of slighter apologies by the aggressor. This is to be determined by the circumstances of the case, but always favourably to the lady.

12. In simple unpremeditated rencontres with the small sword, or couteau-de-chasse, the rule is, first draw, first sheathe; unless blood be drawn; then both sheathe and proceed to investigation.

13. No dumb firing or firing in the air is admissible in any case. The challenger ought not to have challenged without receiving offence, and the challenged ought, if he gave offence, to have made an apology before he came on the ground, therefore children's play must be dishonourable on one side or the other, and is accordingly prohibited.

14. Seconds are to be of equal rank in society with the principals they attend, in as much as a second may either choose or chance to become a principal and equality is indispensable.

15. Challenges are never to be delivered at night, unless the party to be challenged intends leaving the place of offence before morning; for it is desirable to avoid all hot headed proceedings.

16. The challenged has the right to choose his own weapons unless the challenger gives his honour that he is no swordsman, after which, however, he cannot decline any second species of weapon proposed by the challenged.

17. The challenged chooses his ground, the challenger chooses his distance, and the seconds fix the time and terms of firing.

18. The seconds load in the presence of each other, unless they give their mutual honours that they have charged smooth ball and single shot, which shall be held sufficient.

19. Firing may be regulated, first, by signal; secondly by word of command; or thirdly at pleasure, as may be agreeable to the parties. In the latter case, the parties may fire at their reasonable leisure.

20. In all cases a misfire is equivalent to a shot, and a snap or a non-cock is to be considered a misfire.

21. Seconds are bound to attempt a reconciliation before the meeting takes place or after sufficient firing or hits as specified.

22. Any wound sufficient to agitate the nerves and necessarily make the hand shake must end the business for that day.

23. If the cause of the meeting be of such a nature that no apology or explanation can or will be received, the challenged takes his ground and calls on the challenger to proceed as he chooses. In such cases firing at pleasure is the usual practice, but may be varied by agreement.

24. In slight cases the second hands his principal but one pistol, but in gross cases two, holding another case ready charged in reserve.

25. Where the seconds disagree and resolve to exchange shots themselves, it must be at the same time and at right angles with their principles. If with swords, side by side, with five paces' interval.

There were two additional Galway rules:

1. No party can be allowed to bend his knee or cover his side with his left hand, but may present at any level from the hip to the eye.

2. None can either advance or retreat if the ground is measured. If no ground be measured, either party may advance at his pleasure, even to the touch of muzzles, but neither can advance on his adversary after the fire, unless the adversary steps forward on him. N.B. The seconds on both sides stand responsible for this last rule being strictly observed, bad cases having occurred from neglecting it.

   N.B. All matters and doubts not herein mentioned will be explained and cleared up by application to the Committee, who meet alternatively at Clonmel and Galway at the quarter sessions for that purpose.

Despite parliament's previous protestations about making duelling and involvement in it punishable by death, it was quite clearly still commonplace. On Friday, 6 March 1789, an article about duelling appeared in the *Kentish Gazette* concerning a Gustavus Adolphus, who had been the conqueror of the North, and the King of Sweden between 1611 and 1632. He had led his country to military supremacy during the Thirty Years' War between 1618 and 1648, and went on to be regarded as one of the greatest military commanders of all time, with the innovative combined use of the various elements of his army. His most notable victory was in 1631 at the Battle of Breitenfeld, sometimes referred to as the Battle of Leipzig, because of its close proximity to the city. He managed to persuade numerous German protestant states to take the side of Sweden against the armies of the German Catholic League, a masterful stroke in the annals of military history if ever there was one.

The article states:

> Gustavus Adolphus, the conqueror of the North, regarded duelling as the ruin of military discipline. With a view to abolish in his army this barbarous custom, he published an edict, by which the punishment of it was made capital. Sometime after this law had been passed, two officers of superior rank who had a private difference, applied to the King for his permission to decide their quarrel by single combat. Gustavus upon the first blush of their request was fired with indignation. He nevertheless suppressed his feelings, and gave consent, but he annexed to it these conditions; that he should himself

be a spectator of the combat, and should appoint the
time and place.

As soon as I read that caveat I couldn't help but suspect that
wasn't going to be the end of the matter, and that somehow
Gustavus wasn't going to be quite so understanding as it first
might have appeared. I wasn't to be disappointed.

> At the hour prescribed, the King, attended by
> a party of infantry, repaired to the spot, and he
> commanded the troops to form a complete circle
> around the combatants, in the centre of which they
> were to engage. But Gustavus at the time called for
> the Provost Marshal of the Army and gave him the
> express orders; that in the instant one of the parties
> should fall, he should cut off the head of the victor.
> Upon hearing of this terrible resolve of the King,
> the duellists became motionless, but presently
> recollecting themselves and touching with a just sense
> of their flagrant violation or the royal ordinance,
> they threw themselves at the feet of the King, and
> implore his pardon; which having obtained, they
> vowed to each other eternal friendship, and that for
> the time to come they would alone devote their lives
> to the cause and glory of their magnanimous Master.

I imagine that once word of that day's events had filtered back
to camp and the rest of the officers of Gustavus' army, there
were no more requests for permission to have a duel with a
fellow officer. This was obviously a man who didn't want any
of the officers under his command engaging each other in
duelling, regardless of the reason for such an arrangement.

The period of time between the 1700s and 1800s seems to have been a very strange one as far as duelling was concerned. One minute a country talks tough about abolishing the practice by bringing in new measures, rules and laws to put an end to it once and for all, then another article that was written forty or fifty years later, says exactly the same thing, and is still discussing ways to bring it to an end. I am amazed at the number of times I have read about a king or a government issuing a decree, directive or law, banning the practice, in lieu of death, and yet still people carried on duelling.

The *Kentish Gazette* of Tuesday, 15 February 1791 again carried an article with suggestions on how to bring about an end to what was seen as the barbaric practice of duelling, this time put forward by a member of the National Assembly of France. It consisted of six recommendations:

1. That honour as well as virtue, being personal, no citizen can be deprived of it but by his own act, and that it can in no case depend on the caprice of another.
2. That every citizen convicted of having given an affront to another, by words, gestures, or threats, shall be prosecuted, and punished, as a disturber of the public peace.
3. That every person who shall strike another, be declared infamous.
4. That the laws against duelling shall continue in force and be executed with the utmost rigour.
5. That those are to be considered as disgraced, who in contempt of the law dare to give a challenge.
6. That it cannot be dishonourable to refuse a challenge, as true honour consists in submission to the laws.

The *Chester Chronicle* dated Friday, 5 October 1798 included a letter addressed to the editor:

Sir,

At a time when the practice of duelling is so frequent, and particularly amongst military gentlemen, whole services are at this crisis so essential to their country, I think it my duty to transmit to you the following anecdotes. The hint which it offers is salutary, and the narrative may at the same time prove amusing to the numerous readers of the Chester Chronicle.

Two gentlemen, one a Spaniard and the other a German, who were recommended, both by their birth and services, to the Emperor Maximilian the Second, both courted his natural daughter, the fair Helene Schasequinn, in marriage. This Prince, after a long delay, one day informed them, that esteeming them equally, and not being able without some embarrassment to bestow a preference, he should leave it to the force and address of the claimants to decide the question. He didn't mean however, to risk the loss of the one or the other, or perhaps both. He couldn't, therefore, permit them to encounter with offensive weapons, but had ordered a large bag to be produced. It was his decree, that whichever should succeed in putting his rival into this bag should obtain the hand of his daughter.

This singular encounter between the two gentlemen took place in the face of the whole court. The contest lasted for more than an hour. At length the Spaniard yielded, and the German Ebberbard, Baron de Talbert, having planted his rival in the bag, took it upon his back, and very gallantly laid it at the feet of his mistress. It is scarcely necessary to add that he espoused her the next day.

Such sir, is the story, as gravely told by Monsieur de St Foix; and now for my inference. I know not what the feelings of the successful combatant in a duel may be, on having passed a small sword through the body of his antagonist, or a bullet through his thorax; but I am fully of the opinion that he might feel just as much elated, and rather more consoled on having put his adversary into a bag.

This method might have brought an end to the practice of duelling overnight, as win or lose the indignity of rolling on the ground, grappling and wrestling with one another, would have been so unseemly for officers or gentlemen, fear of ridicule would have acted as a deterrent.

An article appeared in the *Sherborne Mercury* of Monday, 24 September 1838, about the King of Naples having issued a decree banning the practice of duelling:

The King of Naples, as we stated the other day, has issued a decree against duelling. The following is a list of its provisions: Every challenge whether verbal or written, shall be punished with imprisonment in the third degree, with incapacity to fill any public function, and with forfeiture of all pensions from two to five years after the expiration of the imprisonment. The same penalties shall be inflicted upon everyone who accepts a challenge. Everyone who insults, strikes or beats another who refuses to accept a challenge, shall be punished according to the existing laws, but in this case the punishment shall be increased one degree. The pains of banishment or imprisonment in irons shall be attended with loss of pensions. If death ensues, the culprit shall be punished with death. If two parties meet and yet no duel takes place, they shall nevertheless be punished with banishment and loss of pensions. If a duel takes place, without either of the combatants being wounded, they shall both receive the punishment of confinement in irons with loss of pensions. If wounds are given, the wounded, if he has not given a wound, shall be punished with confinement in irons and loss of pension, and the party wounding shall be punished according to the maximum of the existing laws.

It would seem the King of Naples was serious in his attempts at banning and outlawing the practice of duelling.

The decree continued:

Death given in a duel shall be punished as murder. The bodies of those who shall be killed in a duel, shall be buried in unconsecrated ground, without any religious ceremony; and no monument shall be erected on the spot. The seconds, bearers of challenges, and all persons who take part in duels, shall be punished according to articles 1, 3, 4, and 5 of this decree. Among military men, as duelling is an act of insubordination, it is punishable by the articles of war, but it shall nevertheless be subject to the provisions of this decree, and in this case the maximum of the penalty applicable shall be raised in one degree, unless it shall thereby involve the pain of death. Banishment and imprisonment shall involve loss of honours and court dignities. All infractions of the laws against duelling shall be referred to the Grand Criminal Court.

The last fatal duel between Englishmen in England took place in 1845, between James Alexander Seton and Henry Hawkey. The dispute between the two men was due to Seton being over familiar with Hawkey's wife.

The background to the affair was that sometime in the early 1840s, James Seton and his wife Susannah moved to Southsea in Hampshire, where they rented rooms. In May 1845, James Seton met a woman by the name of Isabella Hawkey, the wife of a Royal Marines officer, Lieutenant Henry Hawkey. Despite being a married man himself, Seton began pursuing Hawkey's wife, even being as brazen as to visit her at her lodgings whilst her husband was away. On some of these visits, James Seton even brought small presents to give to Isabella. Word of these visits eventually reached Henry Hawkey's ears, and he was understandably not pleased. He forbade his wife from seeing Seton again.

At the time, a weekly ball took place at an establishment known as the King's Rooms in Southsea. On 19 May 1845, Henry and Isabella Hawkey attended the ball, as did James Seton. During the course of the evening, James Seton managed to elicit a dance with Isabella. As soon as this was brought to Hawkey's notice, he flew into a rage and insulted Seton in front of everybody, calling him a blaggard and a scoundrel, although it would appear that Isabella wasn't upset or annoyed by the attention she received from Seton.

After the verbal altercation and whilst maintaining his composure, Seton quietly left the premises and made his way back to his lodgings. Early the next morning, Hawkey was awoken by a naval officer by the name of Lieutenant Rowles, who, acting on behalf of Seton (whom he was second for), issued Hawkey with a formal challenge to a duel. With honour and credibility at stake, Hawkey accepted the challenge. Later that day he purchased a pair of duelling pistols and spent some time practising with them in a gunsmith's that had a shooting gallery within its premises.

Despite having only received the challenge that morning, Hawkey found himself taking part in a duel the same evening. It took place on the beach at Browndown, near Gosport. Both men and their seconds travelled to the beach separately. Hawkey had chosen as his second, Charles Lawes Pym, a lieutenant in the Royal Marines. With both men present, their seconds set out an agreed distance of fifteen paces, leaving Hawkey and Seton to take up their positions, and on an agreed signal, take aim and fire. Seton fired first and missed, whilst Hawkey's pistol, which was half-cocked, failed to fire. With both men's honour still intact, the matter could have ended there. However, having been the one who was challenged, Hawkey had the right to insist on a second exchange of shots, an option which he took. Hawkey's shot struck Seton in the abdomen; Seton didn't return fire. He was carried by his second and followers, placed on a nearby yacht and taken the short distance by sea to Portsmouth. On arrival at the quayside he was transferred to the Quebec Hotel, where he was operated on by Robert Liston, a well-known and well-respected London surgeon. The initial surgery was successful, but unfortunately the wound had become infected, his health deteriorated, and he passed away on 2 June 1845.

Seton's funeral was a grand affair, with nearly all of the town's shops closed as a mark of respect. Many of the townsfolk followed the funeral procession from Southsea to nearby Fordingbridge, where he was buried in the grounds of St Mary's Church.

An inquest into Seton's death opened at Portsmouth Guildhall on 4 June 1845, but it was adjourned on 6 June, before recommencing on 16 June. Henry Hawkey and his second, Lieutenant Charles Lawes Pym were both accused of the wilful murder of Seton, and arrest warrants were issued accordingly.

At the Winchester assizes in March 1846, Lieutenant Pym was charged as an accessory to murder in relation to the death of James Seton, but he was found not guilty and acquitted.

At the Winchester assizes which began on 13 June 1846, Henry Hawkey was tried for the murder of James Seton, a charge that he was found not guilty of. This was mainly down to the adroit oratorical skills of his lawyer, Alexander Cockburn QC, who delivered a two-hour summation, during which he emphasised how his client had been provoked by Seton's continuous and unchivalrous conduct towards his wife. He also made the claim that Seton's death was to a large extent caused by the subsequent medical treatment he received after he had been shot.

There was a certain irony in Hawkey's choice of Cockburn as his lawyer, as he was a renowned womaniser himself.

In 1852, trouble was once again to find its way to Hawkey's doorstep whilst he was still a serving officer in the Royal Marines. Close to the Woolwich Barracks where he was stationed at the time, he attacked a fellow officer, Lieutenant Henry Swain, with his stock and fists; conduct most definitely not becoming of an officer or a gentleman. The attack only came to an end when another Royal Marines officer, who happened to be riding past on his horse, stopped and intervened. Also present was Hawkey's wife, Isabella, who was visibly shocked by the events unfolding in front of her. Both men were subsequently put before a court martial, which resulted in the full facts of the matter coming to light. Lieutenant Swain had been having a sexual affair with Isabella, which was apparently one of the worst-kept secrets of the day; everybody appeared to know about it, including Hawkey himself. Whether he was turning a blind eye to what was going on, or was lying to himself about the dalliance is unclear, but what is clear is that on the day of the assault when he came across Swain in the street, he simply snapped.

During the court proceedings it was revealed that Swain had been paying regular visits to Hawkey's home to see Isabella whilst Hawkey was on duty – a very similar scenario to when Isabella had her affair with James Seton. Swain's affair with Isabella was recounted in vivid detail, which must have been uncomfortable for Hawkey to listen to. One of Hawkey's servants provided evidence to the court that they had walked into the living room unannounced and been confronted by Swain jumping up from the settee, quickly trying to button up his trousers, with Isabella still lying there partly clothed.

Hawkey decided to defend himself rather than acquire a professional legal representative, but he did a decent job. Although he was found guilty of having violently assaulted Lieutenant Swain, he was found not guilty of the more serious charge of 'conduct unbecoming the character of an officer and a gentleman', which meant that his sword was returned to him and that his honour was still intact. To have been found guilty of the latter offence would have left a lifelong scar on his honour.

Once the furore had settled in the weeks after the trial, both Swain and Hawkey were quietly placed on permanent half-pay, which in essence meant they had both been forced into retirement. Although the Royal Marines didn't want the world to know that two of their officers had 'officially' acted in a manner unbecoming their rank and position, they had left a stain on the corps' good name and this was their subtle way of getting their own back on the pair.

Regardless of the outcome of the court martial, Isabella left Hawkey, then divorced him before remarrying a man eleven years her junior. Hawkey died in 1856 of tuberculosis at the age of 39, living a lonely existence in a down-market boarding house, a poorer standard of accommodation than he was used to. It was a sad end for Hawkey and far less dramatic than the short life he had led.

By now there had been a change in the attitude towards duelling, and everything that it represented, even in the military itself, which was surprising. There had been a belief that even officers who were against the idea of duelling had allowed themselves to become embroiled in such events through fear of being labelled a coward if they refused to do so.

Many brave men had lost their lives fighting for, and in defence of, their country, and it was no longer seen to be a noble or honourable act to shoot and kill somebody over what was on most occasions, nothing more than a petty squabble.

A real turning point in the whole practice of duel or no duel was when General Sir Eyre Coote, a battle-hardened soldier who had earned the respect of his fellow soldiers on the battlefield, and was as far from being a coward as it was possible to be, refused to accept a challenge by another officer, instead referring the matter to King George III. Not only did the king fully support Coote by stating that he had acted quite properly, but he also gave the other officer involved a public dressing down – an unpleasant experience for the officer and one which would have harmed his reputation.

The *Hereford Times* of Saturday, 17 January 1846 included an article entitled, 'Duelling – The Anti-Duelling Association':

> In last week's number, we copied from the *Morning Chronicle* a highly interesting article on the Anti-Duelling Association, a pressure of other subjects forced the postponement of a few observations, which we were desirous of offering.
> Having, at an early period of its career, welcomed the establishment of this Association as the nucleus of an ultimate Court of Honour, established under legislative sanction, it is most gratifying to point to that article, wherein is testimony of the thriving condition of the association.
> There are however, two or three points on which we differ from the *Chronicle's* commentary.

The article then included the *Hereford Times'* comment and disagreement on what the *Morning Chronicle* had said in relation to legislation concerning the control of duelling. In essence, the latter had said that direct legislation could do little to cure duelling which was, they said, a moral evil, adding that generally legislation caused more harm than good. The first part of that statement was a stance that the *Hereford Times* vehemently disagreed with, although they appeared to accept that duelling, which was referred to as a social habit, may be such that by meddling directly with it, legislation may do more harm than good. With the benefit of hindsight, I am not sure how that could ever possibly be the case, although the *Hereford Times* did add that the concept would greatly depend upon the 'mode of procedure'.

The Chronicle cited a case in the Royal Navy which had been 'satisfactorily adjudicated, under the new articles of war; and demurs to the opinion of the Committee of the Anti-Duelling Association for suggesting the adoption, in private life, of a similar model of arbitration, on the grounds that there would, in the latter court, be no accredited judge, and besides, people would be averse to referring their private affairs to strangers to whom they owed nothing but a self-imposed allegiance.'

The article continued:

> Now, we take leave to differ widely from our contemporary. The nobleman or gentleman, soldier or sailor, appointed by the Association, would be an accredited judge, what member would refuse to submit his case to this arbitration? Could such a man maintain private or public respect after such repudiation? Out of the society, such an umpire would be most acceptable, and we believe would be preferred by both 'belligerents' to an umpire from among their own acquaintance.
>
> The reasoning, demonstrating the utter absurdity of the practice of duelling, quoted by the *Chronicle* from Mr Knight's Political Dictionary, is truly admirable, it will well repay perusal. Nothing but custom from time immemorial could maintain a practice which is contrary to reason, as it is repugnant to the religious principles of a Christian community.

It is clear to see from this article that by 1846 the practice of duelling was in its final death throes, having become unacceptable to large elements of society.

The following is an article about duelling in England and is taken from the *Sheffield Weekly Telegraph* of Saturday, 20 April 1901:

> In every country of Europe, duelling is forbidden; but there are very few where persons who have a mind to fight seem to be deterred by fear of the legal consequences. Only in England is the custom really disapproved by public opinion, and to say that it may not spring to life here, if fashionable people took it up would be rash.
>
> A good many cartels are delivered in the course of twelve months even now; but one man so foolish as to risk not only hanging or imprisonment, but the mockery of the nation, does not often find another of the same type; and if those two meet, by some rare coincidence, each still has to discover a friend, equally idiotic, who will act as second. The circumstances are quite different elsewhere.

Going by the tone of the words used in the article, it certainly appears that duelling was, if not dead and buried (no pun intended), certainly coming to an end by the turn of the twentieth century. The main reason for its demise appears to have been down to nothing more powerful than the strength of public opinion.

Duelling was about class. It was the domain of the aristocracy and gentlemen. If the common man had a quarrel or disagreement with somebody, they stepped outside and sorted it out with their fists. Punches were thrown by both men as they were cheered on by a large group of alcohol-fuelled friends and colleagues, and when one man was knocked on to his backside, it was usually the end of the matter and the quarrel was deemed to be over. Sometimes the men would retire to the local tavern together for the odd drink or two, either on the house or purchased by a satisfied friend or colleague of one of the men.

The *Telegraph* article continued looking into the history of duelling both in England and abroad. It is interesting to note that duelling came into existence simply because the aristocracy and landed gentry saw the ancient art of fisticuffs being beneath them.

It is good to remember, however, that at various eras of our island story, duelling was as common here as in France or Germany at present, not to say commoner. The movement which put an end to it arose in India. First the Company's Government, and even the Military Authorities, took alarm at a quarrel, it might be called a blood feud, between the Cavalry and Infantry regiments of the Oude Brigade. Fighting was incessant, field officers turn out as eagerly as subalterns, and the General in command declared himself unable to stop the mischief.

The Court of Directors issued an order decreeing that anyone taking part in a duel should cashiered ipso facto. Great was the consternation. But one infantry colonel vowed in public that he would never refuse a challenge, and a cavalry colonel, taking the hint, promptly sent him one. Nearly all the Oude Brigade attended, and saw the latter champion shot dead. Soon after this great scandal, a writer in the *Calcutta Review* alluded to some proceedings of Henry Lawrence, who was young then, but already distinguished. He interpreted the remarks to mean a charge of deliberate falsehood, ascertained the writer's name, and called him out. An explanation settled the matter. But the prospect of a meeting between personages of such standing caused much discussion. General Inglis was to have acted as one of Lawrence's seconds.

This was an excellent example of how class connected the practice of duelling was. It was clear that there was almost more of a macho kudos attached to challenging somebody to a duel, than there was actually going through with it.

The article continued:

Coming home soon afterwards he spoke of the case to his brother, a Member of Parliament, who invited a number of leading personages to his house 'for the purpose of considering the best means to prevent the crime of duelling'. This was in May 1841. The noblemen and gentlemen present, resolved to form an 'Association for the discouragement of duelling,' which held its first meeting at the British Hotel, Cockspur Street, February 12, 1842. In due course a memorial was presented to Her Majesty through the Home Office, signed by 360 personages of the highest distinction. As a result the Articles of War were amended, and then suddenly duelling collapsed. It seems barely credible to us, remembering Sir Henry Lawrence's character and position in later years, that he should have proposed to risk his life, or to take that of another, for an anonymous article in a periodical. But there are cases innumerable more extraordinary. A list of the men who fought duels even in the last century would include most of the famous Statesmen, and not a few of the leading writers.

The above clearly illustrates how duelling had become no more than a badge of honour. Something to brag about at dinner parties or whilst dining at one's club. It made such a man sound like a 'good egg'. It was almost as if to succeed in business or politics, one not only needed to have had a military background, preferably as a cavalry officer, but the added credibility of having challenged someone to a duel, which they had either won, or more importantly hadn't lost.

It is easy to choose the most striking example. Who has not read Macaulay's review of the Life of Mackintosh and laughed over his bitter gibing at the Editor of it? That gentleman did not put his name to the work, he had never been heard of before, nor was he heard of afterwards. There was no need for him to make a personal quarrel of it? But such jeers, unanswerable too, were 'more than flesh and blood could stand', as Macaulay said on one occasion. The victim announced himself, perhaps it is worthwhile to mention that his name was Wallace, and he demanded the life of his traducer. He did not want apologies or explanations. But the astonishing part of the business is that Macaulay never dreamt of refusing him satisfaction, so far as appears. He only asked that combat should be postponed for some reason which escapes our memory, but it was sufficient, infuriated as he was, and thirsting for blood. Mr Wallace accepted it. In his correspondence with friends during the interval, the historian alludes to the impending duel not infrequently, as an engagement certain to come off, and he treats it quite coolly. But delay is perilous in such cases. When the time arrived, Lord Stafford called on Mr Wallace to arrange a meeting; instead of that he arranged terms. The Editor solemnly swore that he had no idea of insulting Mackintosh, and then the critic expressed his regret for saying disagreeable things about the Editor. But when Macaulay was willing to 'go out' what gentleman could refuse?

There was an element of arrogance to it all, where duelling, or rather the challenging of somebody to a duel, had become part of everyday life. It had become a way for a man to earn respect in the eyes of his contemporaries. In some respects it was almost cowardice. Rather than resolve a contested matter by having a physical fight with each other, where there was a clear winner and loser, the upper classes had to go through the pompous pretence of being manly and brave, when really they were being quite the opposite. The surprise is that it went on for so long, but when people lived in a world where they only gravitated towards others who were agreeable to their way of thinking, such behaviour wasn't really surprising.

The *Bolton Evening News* dated Tuesday, 16 January 1906 included the following article about the current state of duelling in Germany, under the headline: 'Official Sanction to Duelling in Germany':

In reply to an interpellation in the Reichstag on Monday on the subject of duelling, the Minister for War read a statement of the Imperial Chancellor, in which the latter said: 'In officers' corps, duelling has been effectively combated by the Emperor's Order of January 1st 1897. A further remedy need only be hoped from a corresponding modification of the provisions of the law. Nevertheless, so long as duelling is widely regarded as a means of redress for injured honour, officers' corps cannot tolerate the presence in their ranks of anybody who is not prepared in a given case to defend his honour with his sword.' This declaration produced considerable sensation.

This article perhaps demonstrates why in the time before the First World War, more German naval officers were killed as a result of duelling than were actually killed at sea.

CHAPTER SEVEN

The French Influence in Duelling

❖

It is noteworthy to mention at this point just how ridiculous the entire practice of duelling was, particularly in France. The last officially recognised judicial duel, which took place in France on 27 November 1386, was between the Norman knight, Jean de Carrouges, who had fought in a number of military campaigns against England and the Ottoman Empire, and the squire and knight, Sir Jack Le Gris.

The background to the duel was an interesting one in that the two men had known each other for many years, certainly as far back as the late 1360s and possibly before that. The men were in fact so close that in 1377, Carrouges made Le Gris godfather to his eldest son, a position of great responsibility and trust at the time. But it would appear that soon after this their friendship began to sour somewhat. That same year, Pierre d'Alençon became the new Count of Perche, after the death of his brother, Robert, for whom Le Gris had served as a man at arms and a squire. Carrouges had also been in his service as a squire.

The demise of the two men's friendship began out of Le Gris's rise under the count, whilst Carrouges was continually overlooked. Things got worse when his wife and son both died in 1380. Soon after this, Le Gris's position under the count was strengthened when, thanks to his literacy and military skills, he remained in his court, whilst Carrouges was sent on a military campaign in Upper Normandy.

While Carrouges was away and anonymous in his absence, Le Gris's stature was still on the rise. Under the friendship of the count, not only had he been introduced at the royal court, he was awarded the prestigious position of royal steward in the royal household of King Charles VI.

Carrouges returned from his military commitments in 1381, along with a new wife, Marguerite de Thibouville, the daughter of a Norman squire. Her father had owned the lands of the domain of Aunou-le-Faucon, which had subsequently been legitimately purchased from him by Count Pierre for a sum of 8,000 livres, four years earlier. Carrouges, for some reason or another, believed he had a right to these lands and wanted them as part of his dowry. This in turn led to arguments, disagreements and Carrouges eventually taking out legal proceedings against the count, matters which Le Gris was also dragged into because of his closeness to the count.

By 1384, Le Gris and Carrouges appeared to have finally settled their differences and were on reasonably good terms with each other, to such an extent that they were both present at the celebrations of the birth of a son to Jean Crispin, a friend of both men. Carrouges took along his wife, Marguerite, who met Le Gris for the first time.

Later that year, Carrouges left to fight in a campaign against the Scots and remained absent from home until 1385. But all wasn't well in his world, even though he was now a knight. He returned in poor health, suffering in part from the rigours of a long and comparatively unsuccessful campaign, only to discover that he was bankrupt.

On 18 January 1386, whilst Carrouges was away in Paris, it is alleged that Le Gris broke into his friend's chateau and in the presence of his squire, a man by the name of Adam Louvel, raped Carrouges' wife, Marguerite. She informed her husband what had happened on his return, thereafter continually pressing him not to let the crime against her go unpunished. Faced with his wife's constant demands on the matter, he presented himself before his master to make his case. This resulted in charges brought against Le Gris with the hearing held in the court of Count Pierre. Unsurprisingly, Le Gris was found not guilty by the count, who was so convinced of his man's innocence that he even accused Marguerite of inventing or dreaming the events which were included in her allegation.

Understandably, Carrouges was far from happy with the outcome of the hearing. He travelled to the Chateau de Vincennes, the court of King Charles VI, just outside Paris, and pleaded with him to be allowed to challenge Le Gris to a judicial duel so that God himself could decide the case. The king decided he would hear the matter before the Parliament of Paris, at the Palais de Justice, on 9 July, before making a decision. As Le Gris was a cleric in minor orders it was also his right to be tried in a church court, one which didn't condone trial by combat. This certainly would have been a safer route to take, because even if he had lost he wouldn't have had to face Carrouges in a duel. However, with honour at stake he opted to face his accusers before the court at the Palais de Justice.

Le Gris and Carrouges faced one another at the Palais de Justice on 9 July 1386, with each man putting his case before the king and his parliament. Carrouges was so determined to have his duel he threw down his gauntlet at the feet of Le Gris, who, regardless of his thoughts on the matter, had no option but to pick it up. Having heard the allegations and counter allegations, the king and his parliament discussed the case in some detail, and determined that the matter would be heard in full, with witnesses giving their evidence in person. If no decision could be reached, then, and only then would the king allow the matter to be decided by a judicial duel, which – to their way of thinking – left it up to God to decide the winner (and ultimately who had been telling the truth).

Le Gris and Carrouges were the first to give evidence, followed by the heavily pregnant Marguerite. Unfortunately for Adam Louvel and Marguerite's servants, in 1386 France, a witness who was deemed to be of low birth had to have the veracity of their evidence tested beforehand by undergoing torture.

After having heard all the evidence, much of it contradictory, parliament was unable to reach a decision. Le Gris's cause wasn't helped when one of the men, Jean Beloteau, who had given him an alibi for one of the nights of the week in question of the alleged rape of Marguerite, was himself arrested for rape in Paris during the trial.

On 15 September 1386, the Parliament of Paris announced that Le Gris and Carrouges would be permitted to take part in a judicial duel, where the two men would fight to the death. The date was set for 27 November 1386, although this was put back to 29 December in order that the king, who was away involved in a campaign in Flanders, could be present to witness it.

There was a lot at stake for both men; one of them would definitely be dead by the end of the duel, and if that was Carrouges, his wife Marguerite would be burned at the stake, as it would have been determined by God that she had lied about her allegation of rape against Le Gris.

The duel took place in the grounds of the Abbey of Saint-Martin-des-Champs in the north of Paris. For his second Carrouges had Waleran III of Luxembourg, Count of Ligny and Saint Pol. As for Le Gris, he had Philip of Artois, Count of Eu.

As if to prove the point that social standing was everything in medieval France, Jacques Le Gris was knighted immediately before the duel. But this wasn't to show him any favour, or even for his own benefit, it was purely to ensure that the social structure was maintained, because if Carrouges, who was already a knight were to lose, it would mean that a man of a lesser rank had defeated somebody above him in status. As far as the French were concerned, this just wouldn't do.

Thousands of people turned up to witness the event. Chroniclers of the day recorded the duel, ensuring there was a written document of this historic occasion. The duel began with both men heavily armoured and on horseback. After charging at each other three times, both men remained astride their horses, although sadly both horses would later die during the fight. Once on foot, each man drew his longsword and quickly advanced, the noise of clashing metal the only sound to be heard as the watching crowds fell silent. Le Gris, being the physically stronger of the two men, pushed home his advantage, stabbing Carrouges through one of his thighs. But his moment of glory, which was sure to follow, never did, because he made a fatal mistake. He withdrew his sword from Carrouges' thigh and stepped back as if to admire what he had done, but because of the weight of his own armour, he stumbled slightly and for a moment was off balance. Without hesitation Carrouges grabbed the lifeline which had presented itself and threw himself at Le Gris, wrestling him to the floor and slashing at him with his own longsword. Although Le

Gris's armour prevented any of the blows from causing any harm, it was also so heavy (with the added weight of Carrouges in his armour sitting astride him) that he was unable to regain his feet. With the use of his longsword, Carrouges smashed open the lock on the faceplate of Le Gris's helmet. The end was near as the silent crowd, nobility and commoner alike, waited in suspense. Carrouges broke the silence by calling upon Le Gris to admit his guilt before he killed him, or risk the flames of hell for his soul. Le Gris replied: 'In the name of God, and on the peril and damnation of my soul, I am innocent of the crime.' Although clear for everyone to hear, it wasn't the answer Carrouges wanted. He drew his misericordia (a long narrow knife specifically used to deliver the death stroke to a knight in battle), and thrust it through Le Gris's throat, killing him instantly.

Carrouges went on to become a wealthy as well as famous individual in the aftermath of his victory, and because of its place in history as the last trial by combat permitted by the Parliament of Paris or a French king, it has remained a point of great interest and debate in France.

The chronicle of the Monk of St Denis, said to have been written by Michel Pintoin (1350-1421) was translated from its original Latin text into French by Belleguet, sometime between 1839 and 1852, some 500 years after the events. Line three of the final paragraph contains the following:

> Afterwards everyone found out who committed the foul rape, when somebody else (person not identified) confessed while being condemned to death.

However, the uncertainty continues. Another chronicler, clergyman Jean Froissart, who was born in the 1330s, relied on first-hand eyewitness accounts for his chronicles. These are recorded and preserved in four books and the account of the duel between Le Gris and Carrouges appears in Book Three. There is no mention of any other person making such a confession.

In the first fourteen years or so of the fifteenth century, it is estimated that some 4,000 French gentlemen lost their lives as a direct result of having been involved in a duel, whilst it was common place for a victorious duellist to be pardoned after having been found guilty in relation a duel-connected 'murder'.

The French nobility were almost looking for reasons to be able to challenge each other to a duel. Although the word honour is often used to justify a duel, it is difficult to reconcile honour with minor disputes such as card games. It was more likely due to a man's reputation in the eyes of his peers; to have been involved in a duel provided the important ingredient of credibility.

During the seventy-two-year reign of Louis XIV of France (1643-1715), many of those who took part in duels were executed for their troubles. It does beg the question: why get embroiled in such a practice in the first place? Still, they did.

Perhaps the strangest French duel that ever took place was in 1808, during the rule of Emperor Napoleon Bonaparte. It involved two French men, Monsieur de Grandpré and a Monsieur le Pique. The dispute on this occasion wasn't over words or a fight, but a woman.

The lady concerned was a noted celebrity of the day, Mademoiselle Tirevit, an opera dancer and a regular performer at the Paris Opera House. She was 'kept' by de Grandpré, but had also become involved with le Pique. Both men weren't just smitten with the woman, but went as far as to declare their love for her. Being unable to decide which of them she wanted to be with, a classic strategy of keeping one's options open, she left it to the two men to sort out, which they did – with a certain amount of panache.

They agreed to resolve their dispute with a duel. This wasn't to be any old duel, facing each other twenty paces apart, armed with a sword or gun. For them, that wasn't grand enough. Instead they came up with the idea of having a balloon duel. A crazy idea where the duel was conducted with each party in a wicker basket suspended under a hot air balloon, hundreds of feet above the ground. It would seem the saying 'love knows no boundaries' included being up in the air for these two Frenchmen.

The date of the duel was set for 3 May 1808 and to ensure that neither man had an unfair advantage, both men constructed identical balloons. On the morning in question, the two men climbed aboard the balloons' baskets, each of them accompanied by their seconds. At 9 am in the Tuileries Garden, a public park between the Louvre and the Place de la Concorde in Paris, the ropes holding the balloons to the ground were cut, and they ascended slowly upwards into the morning skies. The weather was commensurate with the time of year, with a moderate wind blowing in from a north-westerly direction.

The two balloons drew much attention from cheering Parisians out for a morning stroll, or on their way to work, all of them believing they were witnessing nothing more than the beginning of a race. What none of them had seen were the blunderbuss guns that had been carried by both of the seconds. When the balloons reached a height of about half a mile, and were about 250ft apart, which it may be said, is quite a distance, the duel was ready to begin. However, it differed greatly from a duel on the ground. On this occasion the men weren't actually aiming at each other, but at each other's balloons, hence they were using blunderbusses rather than pistols. The effect of a blunderbuss would be much the same as if firing a sawn-off shotgun.

On the setting off of a pre-determined signal from the ground below, the duel commenced. It was le Pique who took the first shot and missed. Bearing in mind the balloons were half a mile up, 250ft apart, the baskets would have been noticeably moving in the wind, making shooting any kind of weapon far from easy. Grandpré took his time, kept calm, aimed the best he could with such a weapon and fired. The shot tore a hole in le Pique's balloon, large enough to have an immediate impact, causing the balloon to quickly collapse and begin to descend, picking up speed as it went. As le Pique and his second plummeted to their deaths, they must have been terrified at the knowledge of their pending doom; it was just a matter of seconds before the basket of their balloon smashed into an unsuspecting Parisian's home.

Le Grandpré and his second celebrated their victory, along with the fact that they were still both alive. Whether Mademoiselle Tirevit was happy with the outcome of the duel, or if she eventually married le Grandpré, is unclear. Whatever the outcome, le Grandpré certainly had an unusual experience. This type of duelling doesn't appear to have become fashionable in France, or any other country for that matter. However, if the story about the French balloon duellists wasn't crazy enough, there is another account of a strange duel, again between Frenchmen, who fought by throwing billiard balls at each other's heads in 1843.

The last fatal duel to have taken place in England was on 19 October 1852, between two French political refugees, Frédéric

Cournet and Emmanuel Barthélemy. The duel took place at Priest Hill near the village of Englefield Green in Surrey, both men having travelled there by train. Who fired first isn't recorded, although both men did discharge their weapons. Cournet missed with his shot, but Barthélemy struck Cournet in his torso. Without stopping to enquire about his opponent's wellbeing, Barthélemy and his two seconds immediately left the scene to catch a train back to London's Waterloo railway station. As for Cournet, one of his seconds fled the scene in a blind panic, whilst the other remained by his side to comfort his badly wounded friend with nothing more potent than kind words; not being a doctor, there was little else he could do. By sheer luck and coincidence, the first man to come across them was a local doctor. The two men carried the wounded Cournet to the nearby Barley Mow pub and notified the local police of his condition and that the opponent and his seconds were en route for London. Acting quickly, the Surrey Police sent a message to their Metropolitan Police colleagues by telegraph. They reached Waterloo station before the train arrived, and arrested the three Frenchmen as they stepped on to the platform.

Cournet died some hours after being shot and was buried at St John's Church, Egham. Barthélemy, his two seconds, along with Cournet's second, were all charged with murder at the Kingston assizes on 21 March 1853 and were all found guilty of manslaughter, not murder. By the time the matter came to court, they had already been in prison for five months. All four men were faced with a further two months in prison.

Although it seems Barthélemy challenged Cournet to a duel because of offensive remarks he had made about a former girlfriend of his, the duel may have been more politically motivated. Despite politically being on the far left, both men were part of different factions, with Barthélemy being a follower of Louis Blanqui, and Cournet favouring the views of Alexandre Auguste Ledru-Rollin, a French politician who fought for the working classes and was forced into exile after the failure of the 1848 French Revolution.

After his spell in prison, Barthélemy began working as an engineer for a man called George Moore, whose business was in soda water. Moore lived in Warren Street, London, and on the evening of 8 December 1854 he was visited by Barthélemy and an unknown woman. Although the evening began with the normal social pleasantries expected of such a soirée, it didn't end on friendly terms. For some reason, the two men got into a quarrel that ended in Barthélemy beating Moore with a stick, before shooting him dead. Just as Barthélemy was leaving Moore's house, a neighbour, Charles Collard, who was an ex-policeman and who had heard the gunshot, attempted to detain Barthélemy, but was shot and wounded in the attempt. Barthélemy ran off but was chased and apprehended by a passing member of the public; his female companion managed to escape and was never seen again.

Collard died from his wounds the next day, but not before he had identified Barthélemy as the man who had shot him. Barthélemy went to trial on 4 January 1855, but only for the killing of Charles Collard. For some unknown reason, he wasn't charged in relation to the murder of George Moore. He was found guilty Collard's murder, but with a recommendation from the jury that he be shown mercy. But the two judges took no heed of what the jury had to say, and sentenced him to death. After he was convicted, Barthélemy gave an account of what happened between him and Moore, saying that they had quarreled over money Moore owed to the woman who was with him. He claimed that his shooting of Moore was purely accidental and happened whilst he was struggling with him when attempting to escape. In the circumstances, he had nothing to gain from lying, since the death sentence had already been passed.

Barthélemy was hanged on the morning of Monday, 22 January 1855, at Newgate Prison in the City of London. His last request was to hold a piece of paper in his hand whilst being hanged. This turned out to be a letter, written in French, from a woman named Sophie. The speculation by many on hearing this news was that this was the same woman who was with Barthélemy at the time he shot Moore.

Saturday, 15 January 1870, saw an article appear in the *Leicester Mail* about another duelling incident which had taken place in Paris on Monday, 10 January. It tells of an incident involving a nephew of Napoleon Bonaparte.

> The late editions of the evening papers announce a tragedy which has taken place at the house of Prince Pierre Bonaparte. This relative of the second Caesar has shot at and killed Monsieur Victor Noir, a journalist. Prince Pierre is the fourth son of Lucien Bonaparte, the brother of the first Napoleon. He was born in 1815, and has gained some reputation as an energetic character, passing through many phases of life in America, Italy and Belgium, and finally settling in France, after the expulsion of Louis Philippe. The pen of Rochefort, which never yet spared a Napoleon, has at length reached Pierre.
>
> An insulting article in the new journal of the Paris deputy, *La Marseillaise,* drew forth a challenge form the Prince. The letter in which this defiance was conveyed is a smart specimen in its way.

'It is quite natural,' says the Prince, 'that after insulting every other member of the Bonaparte family, Rochefort should give the remaining one a turn. But I have this advantage over most of those who bear my name. I am a private individual, though a Bonaparte. I proceed to enquire then, if you are prepared to defend with your breast the effusions of your pen; though I confess that I have little confidence in the result of my request. In fact I learn from the newspapers that your electors have given you the imperative mandate to refuse all honourable satisfaction, and to preserve your previous existence. Nevertheless I venture to make the experiment in the hope that some feeble vestige of French sentiment will induce you to make one exception in my favour from those measures of prudence and precaution in which you have taken refuge. If, peradventure, you consent to relax the conditions which render your honourable person doubly inviolable, you will find me neither in palace nor chateau, but simply at 59 Rue d'Auteuil; and I promise that if you present yourself, you will not be confronted by a "Not at home".'

Powerful words indeed and not ones that the intended recipient, journalist Henri Rochefort, who was also the founder of the newspaper *La Marseillaise*, could ignore.

What happened after Rochefort received this communication isn't clear, but it was rumoured that Victor Noir had attended Prince Bonaparte's home at Rue d'Auteuil in Paris whilst acting as Rochefort's second, to arrange the details of a duel between the two men. At that meeting, Noir informed Prince Bonaparte that it was he who was in fact the author of the article in *La Marseillaise* that he had been offended by, and offered to take the duel himself, an offer that was refused. Noir was then said to have reacted by assaulting the prince and was shot dead for his troubles.

Whether that version of events is correct is unclear because Prince Bonaparte also had a quarrel with Monsieur Paschal Grousset, the journalist who actually wrote the offending article. The 'other' version is that Noir was at Prince Bonaparte's home, not as the second for Rochefort but Grousset. This was confirmed when a telegram, which had been sent by Grousset and published in another Parisian newspaper, spoke of the death of his second.

In essence there is part truth in both those accounts. Grousset had in fact sent Noir and a Monsieur Ulric Fonvielle to speak with Prince Bonaparte. When the two men arrived at his house they were ushered into the drawing room, where they presented the prince with a letter signed by Grousset. The prince declined his challenge stating that he would fight Rochefort not his 'menials'. Noir responded by striking the prince violently in the face, although Fonvielle would later claim it was the prince who struck Noir in the face before shooting him. Fonvielle, possibly in a bit of a panic, pulled out a revolver but didn't fire. The prince grabbed for a nearby pistol of his own and shot Noir, wounding him. The latter staggered to the bottom of the stairs, where he died. Meanwhile, Fonvielle quickly left the premises.

Prince Bonaparte was arrested on suspicion of the murder of Noir, with the full approval of the emperor, and tried for homicide in at the High Court convened in the city of Tours on 21 May 1871. The man in charge of proceedings was the attorney general of France, Théodore Grandperret, a staunch supporter of the Bonaparte family. The prince's subsequent acquittal didn't come as a surprise to many.

CHAPTER EIGHT

Duelling Anecdotes

❖

A Strange Duel

A duel took place in Siam in 1593 between the Siamese King, Naresuan, and the Burmese Crown Prince, Mingyi Swa, which was won by King Naresuan. What I found particularly interesting about it was the fact that it was conducted whilst both men were astride elephants!

Frederick the Great

Frederick the Great ruled the Kingdom of Prussia between 1740 and 1786, with his greatest achievements during those forty-six years being many military victories, including his success, against great odds, in the Seven Years' War between 1756 and 1763.

He was so opposed to the practice of duelling he decided he was going to put a stop to it once and for all – at least in his army. He issued an order that the first men who engaged in a duel without his personal consent would be summarily punished. The day after his order had been issued, he was approached by one of his officers who asked for his permission to challenge a fellow officer to mortal combat. He gave his consent, but stipulated that he should be notified beforehand of the time and location of where the duel was to be fought.

This request was adhered to, and when the belligerent parties arrived to fight their duel they found their king waiting for them. To their great surprise they saw a gibbet erected in the centre of the area where they were due to fight. The officer who had requested permission from the king for the duel to take place respectfully asked him what this spectacle was all about.

'It means this,' answered the king sternly, 'I intend to witness your battle until one of you has killed the other, and then I will hang the one who survives.' Not surprisingly, the duel didn't take place. After that date duelling became an extremely rare event in Frederick the Great's army.

Judge Thatcher of Maine

The late Judge Thatcher of Maine was a member of Congress between 4 March 1789 and 3 March 1801. During his period of office, he was challenged to a duel by a fellow congressman. The judge was certainly not lacking in basic animal courage, but despite his ability to look after himself, he was vehemently opposed to the practice of duelling. The following response was only to be expected from such a man:

'I will go and consult with my wife; and if she consents, be sure I will accommodate you.'

The challenger replied, 'Ha! You are a coward.' To which Thatcher replied. 'Aye, you thought I was, or you never would have challenged me.'

Marquis de Donnisau

In the memoirs of the Marquis de Donnisau, who was totally against duelling, he wrote the following passage:

One day he overheard two brave soldiers, belonging to his cavalry, just winding up a heated and angry dispute by drawing their swords for mortal combat. The challenge had been given, and instantly accepted. 'Hold one moment!' the Marquis exclaimed, as he came upon the scene. 'Which of you two, think ye, will have the pleasure of robbing himself of a friend and a brother, and at the same time robbing me of one of my best and bravest soldiers? Have we no enemies, that you must turn your swords against one another?'

For a time the two soldiers could only stand and stare at the ground, evidently feeling foolish. Eventually they put away their swords, shook hands and thanked the marquis for the lesson he had taught them.

Stephen Decatur Jr.

Stephen Decatur Jr. began his distinguished career in the US navy in 1798 at the age of 19. From his entry as a midshipman he eventually reached the rank of commodore, the same as his father Stephen Decatur Sr. He was what would be by today's standards termed as a 'flyer', reaching the rank of captain by the age of 25, which to this day makes him the youngest man to have reached that rank in the history of the US navy. The down side of his meteoric rise through the ranks was jealousy on the part of a number of contemporaries who had been much older by the time they had attained the same rank.

Decatur was noted as being brave and heroic as well as a natural leader who cared greatly for those under his command. His naval service saw him involved in the Quasi War with France between 1798 and 1800, the Barbary Wars (off North Africa) between 1801 and 1805, and the War of 1812 with the British, all of which saw him deliver a number of victories, not only elevating his own personal standing but that of the US navy as a major power on the high seas.

Decatur's naval career (and his life) was cut short when he was shot and killed during a duel with fellow commodore, James Barron, on 22 March 1820. The two men fought each other over remarks Decatur had made about Barron, and his conduct in the 1807 Chesapeake-Leopald affair. Barron made the challenge after Decatur had refused to withdraw his remarks.

Regardless of how Decatur felt about his duel with Barron, maybe he was reminded of the time he had acted as a second to his friend Oliver Hazard Perry in a duel against Captain John Heath, who was in charge of the Marines on board USS *Java*, on which both men served. On the day of that duel in October 1818, Heath had fired first and missed, while Perry refused to return fire. That was the end of the matter with both men happy that their honour had been satisfied.

In the Chesapeake-Leopald incident of Monday, 22 June 1807, Commodore James Barron was in charge of the USS *Chesapeake*, when an engagement began with the Royal Naval vessel, HMS *Leopard*. After being pursued and attacked with broadsides and only firing once in response, James Barron surrendered his vessel to the British and allowed them to board his ship. Having carried out a search of the vessel, the British, who were looking for deserters from the Royal Navy, removed four of the *Chesapeake's* crew, before allowing her to continue on her way. On arriving back in the United States, Barron was relieved of his command and court martialled.

Decatur had been one of the senior officers on the board at Barron's court martial, at which time he was found guilty of 'unpreparedness' and banned from any future command for a period of five years from that date. Soon after this Barron left the US and made his way to Copenhagen, where he remained for six years and sought re-instatement to the US navy, one would assume at his previous rank. This wasn't popular amongst his fellow naval officers, and one of the most outspoken of his detractors was none other than Stephen Decatur, by then on the United States Board of Naval Commissioners.

This ultimately resulted in the duel between the two men taking place. Although duelling still occurred in America, due to the number of experienced men the US navy had lost in this manner it was a practice which the navy didn't welcome. Any officer who went through with a duel and survived ran the risk of being discharged from the service.

As was the custom, each man had a nominated second. Decatur had asked his friend and fellow naval officer Thomas Macdonough to fulfil this role, but he politely refused on the grounds that he had always openly opposed duelling. Macdonough had achieved his own fame and glory when he commanded American naval forces during the War of 1812, defeating the British at the Battle of Lake Champlain and helping bring an end to the war. Decatur then turned to Commodore William Bainbridge. As for Barron, he chose Captain Jesse Elliot, who was no great fan of Decatur.

The duel took place on 22 March 1820 at the Bladensburg duelling grounds, not far outside Washington. Barron had spoken to Decatur of conciliation on that very morning, but there was no attempt to explore this avenue. Decatur had proved himself to be an excellent shot with a pistol, but was only intending to wound Barron. However, intending to hit an adversary in a certain part of his anatomy and actually managing to do it during the pressure of a duel, are two different matters. Missing one's point of aim by just a matter of inches could mean the difference between life and death.

Any duel has its dangers, which was added to the closer the men stood to each other. One of the usual ways a duel was staged was for the men to start off standing back-to-back and, on a given signal, walk for a distance of twenty paces before turning, facing their adversary, taking aim and firing. On this occasion the two men began by facing each other at a distance of eight paces, or about 24ft away from each other. According to reports on the events of that day, Decatur's second, Bainbridge, gave the following instruction to both men:

'I shall give the word quickly. "Present, one, two, three." You are neither to fire before the word "one", nor after the word "three".'

With both men in position, they raised and cocked their weapons, took aim at each other, and waited with bated breath for Bainbridge to begin. As soon as he called out 'one', both men fired almost simultaneously; each of the shots hit their mark, and both men fell to the floor. Barron's shot hit Decatur in the pelvic area, with Decatur hitting Barron in the lower abdomen, which then in turn ricocheted into one of his thighs.

Decatur was carefully lifted into the carriage of one of his supporters, Commodore John Rodgers, and taken back to his home at Lafayette Square in Washington, where he was attended to by a number of physicians. For some unknown reason, even though it had been located Decatur refused to allow the ball to be removed from his wound. Unfortunately for him the round had also cut through some of his arteries, and with medical science nowhere near as advanced as it is today, he was never going to survive such internal damage, even though the wound itself was non-life threatening. He died later that evening.

His funeral was a grand affair, with a crowd estimated to have been somewhere in the region of 10,000. Such was Decatur's fame and stature in American society, the President of the United States, James Munroe attended, as well as most of the members of Congress, along with numerous other dignitaries of the day. Decatur's body was initially interred in the Barlow family vault at Kalorama, Washington, at the behest of his widow, Susan, although it is unclear what connection either of them had with the Barlow family. In 1946, his remains were moved to Philadelphia, where he was buried at St Peter's Churchyard, next to the grave of his parents.

As for James Barron, he was never prosecuted over the death of Stephen Decatur. He remained in the navy but on shore duty. In 1839 he became the United States' most senior officer. He died at the age of 82, on 21 April 1851 in Norfolk, Virginia.

Otto von Bismarck

In early June 1865, Otto von Bismarck, at the time Minister President in the German Landtag (Parliament), challenged Rudolf Virchow to a duel after the two men clashed over the topic of funding for the navy. In keeping with the rules, Virchow was allowed to choose the weapons that the pair would fight with. Rather than choose swords or pistols, as one might expect when considering such an eventuality, he chose two large sausages, one each for both of them to eat, but one of them was to be infected with *Trichinella*, a roundworm.

The larvae invade the body's muscle tissue and the symptoms include fever, malaise and oedema. It isn't usually fatal, but leaves a victim with muscle pain and weakness.

Having given the idea some thought, von Bismarck declined, and no duel between the two men took place. Some years before this, possibly in about 1852, when von Bismarck was a Prussian envoy working in Frankfurt, he became involved in an argument with Georg von Vinck, a Prussian politician, which resulted in a duel taking place between the two men, but neither of them were hurt in the exchange.

CHAPTER NINE

Miyamoto Musashi – Japanese Samurai Warrior

❖

No book on duelling would be complete without a chapter on samurai warriors. The first traces of the samurai warrior clans can be traced back to the end of the eighth century. They spent the next 400 years consolidating their position, strengthening their power base as both warlords and land owners.

From the thirteenth century, a samurai warrior's primary weapon became the now world-famous samurai sword, which was treated with a certain spiritual reverence by those who earned the right to possess one. At around the same time there had been a change for samurai warriors, in that they began to move away from fighting on horseback where their favoured weapon was the bow and arrow.

To be a samurai warrior, a man was expected to live by an ethical code of conduct. This was known as Bushido, which in English simply means, 'Way of the Warrior'. A samurai worked for a 'Lord' to whom they would be expected to give their complete loyalty and be willing to die for if the need arose. In return they would be suitably compensated with both land and money. But for most samurai, their actions were about honour, exactly the same as it was for those involved in duelling throughout Europe and America.

Quite possibly the most famous of the samurai was Miyamoto Musashi, who was born in 1584 and lived until he was about 60. It is said that he fought and remained undefeated throughout his sixty-one duels, some of which were duelling in its rawest form, because it was very likely that death to one man would be through decapitation – although not all duels were with swords and, unless it had been agreed beforehand that it was to be a fight to the death, not all participants tried to kill their opponent.

Musashi fought his first duel when he was just 13 years old. A passage in the 2004 book, *The Lone Samurai*, by William Scott Wilson, included the following about this duel:

> In 1596, Musashi was 13, and Arima Kihei, who was traveling to hone his art, posted a public challenge in Hirafuku-mura. Musashi wrote his name on the challenge. A messenger came to Dorin's temple, where Musashi was staying, to inform Musashi that his duel had been accepted by Kihei. Dorin, Musashi's uncle, was shocked by this, and tried to beg off the duel in Musashi's name, based on his nephew's age. Kihei was adamant that the only way his honour could be cleared was if Musashi apologised to him when the duel was scheduled. So when the time set for the duel arrived, Dorin began apologising for Musashi, who merely charged at Kihei with a six foot quarterstaff, shouting a challenge to Kihei. Kihei attacked with a wakizashi, but Musashi threw Kihei on the floor, and while Kihei tried to

get up, Musashi struck Arima between the eyes and then beat him to death. Arima was said to have been arrogant, overly eager to battle, and not a terribly talented swordsman.

One particular series of duels against members of the same family stands out.

On 8 March 1604, Musashi took part in a duel against Yoshioka Seijuro on the outskirts of Kyoto. Seijuro was the master of the Yoshioka Sword Fighting School in the city and accepted Musashi's challenge. The agreement between the two men had been for only one blow each. Musashi struck first, his blow catching Seijuro on his left shoulder. It was so powerful that it knocked him out and badly damaged his arm.

Once again the word honour entered the affray and Seijuro's brother, Yoshioka Denshichiro, immediately challenged Musashi to a duel in an effort to take revenge for what he had done to Seijuro. The chosen location for the duel was outside of the Sanjusangen-do Buddhist temple in Tokyo. As he had been for the duel against Seijuro, Musashi was late, perhaps a tactic on his part to enrage his opponent and hope that in doing so, he would lose his focus.

Denshichiro's choice of weapon was a long wooden staff, which had some kind of steel attachment. Musashi was armed with no more than a bokken, or a wooden sword, which confused and annoyed Denshichiro as they had agree that it was to be a fight to the death. However, regardless of the weapon he had, Musashi defeated and killed Denshichiro with consummate ease. It took only seconds for Musashi to strike Denshichiro with an instantly fatal blow to the head. The Yoshioka home and school now passed to 12-year-old brother, Yoshioka Matashichiro.

One might think that after having lost two prominent members of his family in duels with Musashi, Matashichiro would have drawn a line in the sand and moved on. But that wasn't to be the case, as still the Yoshioka family sought the death of Musashi and the reclamation of their family honour. A fight between Musashi and a 12-year-old boy was never going to be a fair contest, but Musashi was challenged to a duel, and once again he accepted. This time the location was to be near to Ichijo-ji Temple, just outside Kyoto.

Even though he was only 12 years old, Matashichiro was now the leader of the Yoshioka clan and regardless of what he felt about the situation, he had no option but to challenge Musashi. He did so, but requested that the duel take place at night, immediately raising Musashi's suspicions. However, he agreed to the condition. Despite usually turning up late for such meetings, to be on the safe side Musashi turned up for this duel hours earlier than he needed to, hid himself away and sat and waited to see what would unfold.

Matashichiro arrived with a small army of archers, musketeers and swordsmen, who kept out of sight so that it appeared that he was on his own. It was a trap, with himself as the bait. Seeing this, Musashi dashed out from his hiding place, and before any of Matashichiro's entourage could react, he got to him and killed him by cutting off his head, then whilst making good his escape, he fought off his would-be killers by fighting with a sword in each hand, before he could be overpowered and killed. This was a manner of fighting that had never been seen before, and went on to become known as the *Niten Ichi-ryū* sword style. It was specifically intended to deal with being attacked from all sides at the same time.

What is even more remarkable about Musashi's victories against the Yoshioka family was that he was only 22 years old at the time. He was probably born with great talent and simply honed his skills to perfection.

Musashi would, and did, fight anybody, because he wasn't afraid of them. Size, age or ability of his opponents didn't deter him as he had absolute belief in his own capabilities.

Sasaki Kojiro was known as 'The Demon of the Western Provinces', with his weapon of choice being a *no-dachi* or a long *kotana*, what would be recognised today as a traditional Japanese samurai sword. To give it a European comparison would be to put it up against a longsword or a claymore, commonplace choice of weapons during medieval times.

Sasaki was a formidable opponent, possibly the most skilled that Musashi had ever fought, and was considered by many as a master swordsman. He was most definitely not a lesser samurai's first choice of whom they would want to fight against, especially if it was a fight to the death.

When talking about such events that took place more than 400 years ago, it is difficult to be completely certain about the accuracy, as over time the account of the incident may have been re-written many times. Source documents no longer exist, and different historians will interpret or translate words and documents differently, which can change the meaning of what actually took place. Even with source documents from that period, consideration has to be given to who wrote them and why. There was no such thing as freelance journalism in early seventeenth-century Japan. Chroniclers of the time who recorded events that displeased the people they were ultimately responsible to, may have been put to death.

The facts as can be best determined are that Musashi had heard of Sasaki's well-earned reputation, and deeming him to be a worthy opponent, arranged a duel with him through an intermediary of Lord Hosokawa Tadaoki. The two men met each other on 13 April 1612, on the beach at the island of Ganryu-jima, a strait between Honshu and Kyushu, with the outcome of the fight being a victory for Musashi. Once again he used his seemingly deliberate annoying tactic of turning up late. If it was an intentional tactic, it was certainly an effective one, as his irritated opponent didn't have a clear focus on the contest.

This is an event that took place more than 400 years ago, so it is of no surprise that during this time there have been different versions of what actually happened. Here is my favourite account:

Sasaki Kojiro, who was thought of by many as the best samurai in the whole of Japan, saw Musashi's conduct and behaviour in keeping him waiting as being both insulting and disrespectful. Sasaki was unusual in that his preferred weapon of choice was a sword called the *no-dachi,* a large, and some would say, a slightly unsubtle weapon and one which was readily distinguishable because of its curved blade. If Sasaki's choice of weapon was unusual, then Musashi's use of his *bokken*, was somewhat unbelievable. He used it regardless of what weapon the man he was fighting against possessed.

Kojiro's supporters, including servants, friends, students, and even cooks, along with a number of local officials, arrived by boat early on the morning of the fight. They set a small fire to make a meal and some tea, mainly so that the dignitaries could watch and enjoy the fight in comfort. Kojiro had risen early, around 3 am, beginning his day in deep meditation before joking with his friends and engaging the officials in polite conversation, whilst taking a little tea. He remained calm and relaxed, leaving his friends confident in their belief that he would win the day.

But as the morning turned in to the afternoon, so Kojiro's demeanour changed. He was no longer composed, instead becoming agitated and annoyed, pacing up and down the beach. It had even been suggested by one of the officials that maybe Musashi had backed out of the fight and wasn't coming, but Kojiro knew that wasn't the case. In fact, Musashi wasn't that far away. He was in a nearby inlet, seated in a small fishing boat, off to the south of the beach where he had kept Kojiro waiting. Musashi had spent his time well, sitting quietly with the boat's owner, an old, wrinkled fisherman. Using a sharp knife, he had spent most of the morning shaping a spare oar in to a perfectly balanced *bokken*.

He didn't look as one might expect of such a talented swordsman. For him there was no set of fine clothes, only a stained and, in parts, discoloured robe, and a sword belt. Physically he wasn't what might have been expected of a master samurai. Not particularly tall, and a slenderly built man, he was unshaven, his skin was pale, and his scruffy bundle of hair was tied in a functional bun on the top of his head. His appearance certainly didn't scream out 'samurai'. He looked more like a commoner if one had to describe him in any particular way. The only part of him that caught the eye were a pair of *katana* swords tucked in to his belt, their well-polished sheaths noticeable in the midday sun.

When he was ready, Musashi had the fisherman slowly row him to the beach where Kojiro was waiting somewhat impatiently. Such was Musashi's appearance and demeanour that as the small fishing boat approached, Kojiro didn't immediately recognise him, but when he did, he was enraged. He couldn't believe that a fellow samurai could behave in such a manner, which he took as an insult to his honour. His anger and rage at being kept waiting by Musashi all morning could be held back no more. With his *no-dachi* sword in his hand, he focused his anger and rushed down the beach to engage Musashi in mortal combat. Musashi stepped from the fishing boat in to the waiting surf, but drew neither of the *katana* swords from his belt, instead he was already armed with his freshly made *bokken*. Kojiro was momentarily confused and lost his concentration as he struggled to grasp how any opponent, regardless of who they were, would face him armed with only a *bokken*. Was it arrogance, stupidity or an act of madness, he couldn't decide. He swung his powerful sword towards Musashi, who managed to avoid the intended blow, but only just, as the blade of Kojiro's *no-dachi* sword flew just over his head.

Musashi swung his *bokken*, catching Kojiro on his right side, knocking the wind out of him in the process. Kojiro swung his sword wildly, hitting nothing but thin air, and before he could regain his composure he had been struck twice more, once to the side of the head followed by a powerful blow to his left side, which cracked a number of his ribs. He fell to the sand, quickly finding himself in a world of pain as the life drained out of his body.

The duel between the two great warriors was over in no more than a matter of seconds. Musashi, his work done, bowed to his dying opponent in an act of respect, before returning to his boat and leaving.

It would be fair to say that Miyamoto Musashi had a major influence on future generations of martial arts enthusiasts from all over the world. In Japan he was revered as a *kensai*, which in English literarily translates into 'sword saint'.

Musashi was most definitely a very famous samurai warrior and undoubtedly a gifted and skilled fighter. Whether he was the greatest swordsman of all time would be a matter of opinion.

CHAPTER TEN

Duels Across Time

❖❖❖

This chapter lists just some of the known duels or gunfights, which took place during the eighteenth and nineteenth centuries, throughout the US, Italy, France, Germany and the UK. Although duels did take place in other countries, including Argentina, Australia, Canada, Chile, China, Japan, Malta, New Zealand, Philippines, Portugal, Russia, Siam, Spain, Sweden, Switzerland, Turkey, and Uruguay, this list is of the more significant ones.

Significant Duels in the US

16 May 1777. Button Gwinnett, one of the men who signed the American Declaration of Independence, had a duel with his political opponent, Lachlan McIntosh; both men were wounded, but Gwinnett died three days later.

24 November 1801. Philip Hamilton, son of former United States Secretary of the Treasury, fought a duel against a man by the name of George Eacker, and was killed.

12 August 1817. Thomas Hart Benton and Charles Lucas, who were the prosecution and defence attorneys in a court case, fought each other in a duel on the famous Bloody Island.

Lucas was shot in the throat and Benton in the leg, both men survived.

27 September 1817. Benton and Lucas fought each other in a duel for a second time, once again on Bloody Island. Benton challenged Lucas after he had said that the first fight was unfair because the pair were 30ft apart, and as Benton was a better shot this gave him an advantage. This time they faced each other at just 9ft distance. Benton, who was uninjured, shot and killed Lucas.

30 June 1823. Joshua Barton and Thomas C. Rector fought each other in a duel on Bloody Island. It came about because Barton's brother, Senator David Barton, had sought to block the reappointment of Rector's brother, William, to the position of surveyor general for Missouri, Illinois, and Arkansas. Barton was killed whilst Rector remained uninjured.

26 April 1826. Henry Clay and John Randolph, fought each other in a duel at Pimmit Run, Virginia, fortunately both men were poor shots.

22 September 1826. US representative Sam Houston of Tennessee severely wounded General William A. White in a pistol duel near Franklin, Kentucky. The duel came about as a result of a disagreement over the political appointment of the Nashville Postmaster.

19 September 1827. A duel took place between Samuel Levi Wells III and Dr Thomas Harris Maddox, which then turned into a brawl involving notable figures such as Jim Bowie, who was badly wounded as a result of the fight.

25 January 1828. George W. Crawford, who at the time was the attorney general for the state of Georgia, killed Thomas E. Burnside, who was the Georgia state legislator in a duel. Crawford had challenged Burnside after he had published written defamation about Crawford's father.

26 August 1831. Thomas Biddle and Missouri Congressman Spencer Darwin Pettis fought a duel on Bloody Island. Biddle had challenged Pettis because of comments he had made about Biddle's brother, who was president of the United States bank. Both men were mortally wounded after firing at each other whilst standing just 5ft apart.

10 August 1832. Savannah physician Philip Minis shot and killed Georgia State Legislator James Stark, after which Minis claimed that a valid duel had occurred. Minis also claimed his right to self-defence, saying he hadn't agreed to the duel and that he shot Stark to save his own life. A jury found Minis not guilty.

25 September 1832. A duel took place between James Westcott, a Democratic Party politician and Thomas Baltzell, a lawyer and politician. Baltzell was uninjured whilst Westcott was injured but survived and went on to become a United States senator.

5 February 1837. Texan Brigadier General Albert Sidney Johnston was shot in a duel with Felix Huston over a military position.

24 February 1838. William Jordan Graves, a US representative from Kentucky, fought Johnathon Cilley, a US representative from Maine in a pistol duel. After the duel, the American

Congress passed a law making it illegal to issue or accept a duel challenge in Washington DC.

12 December 1839. Florida Militia Brigadier General Leigh Read and Colonel Augustus A. Alston, a Whig Party leader, fought each other in a duel using rifles whilst standing just fifteen paces apart.

Read had been challenged twice by Alston, who was an overconfident duellist, and somewhat unexpectedly, Read killed him.

26 July 1847. Albert Pike and John Selden Roane fought each other in a duel. Both men discharged their weapons but neither of them were wounded. It was therefore declared a draw.

1 June 1853. US Senator William McKendree Gwin fought a duel against US Congressman J.W. McCorkle. Neither man sustained any injuries.

26 August 1856. Benjamin Gratz Brown and Thomas C. Reynolds fought each other in a duel on Bloody Island. Brown was then the abolitionist editor of the *St Louis Democrat* and Reynolds was a pro-slavery district attorney from St Louis. Brown was shot in the leg, which caused him to limp for the rest of his life, while Reynolds was unhurt.

Brown later became the Union-sanctioned governor of Missouri, whilst Reynolds became a Confederate governor of Missouri.

13 September 1859. A duel took place between United States Senator David C. Broderick and the former chief justice of the Supreme Court of California, which resulted in Broderick being shot dead.

6 September 1863. Brigadier General Lucius Marshall Walker, the nephew of the then President James K. Polk, and General John Sapington Marmaduke, the future governor of Missouri, fought a duel because of differences they had at the battles of Helena and Reed's Bridge in Arkansas. Both men missed their first shots, but Marmaduke mortally wounded Walker with his second shot. Walker died the next day.

22 July 1867. John Bull killed Langford Peel in a quick-draw duel in Salt Lake City, Utah. Peel challenged Bull after the two had argued about their business, which resulted in Peel slapping Bull round the face. Confusion reigned about whether a challenge had been laid down, which was made worse because Bull didn't have a gun. Peel told him to go and get his own gun and come back. Peel waited in the saloon for Bull for more than an hour, but when he failed to turn up, Peel left, not knowing that Bull hadn't turned down his challenge, but was just late. They met up again in another saloon, where the two drew their weapons and Bull shot Peel dead.

9 March 1877. Gamblers Jim Levy and Charlie Harrison got into a disagreement in a saloon in Cheyenne, Wyoming. Levy challenged Harrison to continue their argument outside, Harrison agreed, and the two squared off in the street. During the duel, Harrison fired wildly, whilst Levy took careful aim, fired and shot Harrison.

7 June 1882. Louisiana State Treasurer Edward A. Burke fought a duel with pistols against C. Harrison Parker, who was the editor of the New Orleans *Daily Picayune*. The contest came about after Parker had published some unflattering remarks about Burke, who in turn challenged him to a duel.

8 February 1887. A quick-fire duel took place in Fort Worth, Texas, between Jim Cartwright and Luke Short, which resulted in Cartwright being killed.

Significant Duels in Great Britain and Ireland

December 1597. Sir William Brooke, the son of William Brooke, 10th Baron of Cobham, was fatally wounded in a duel with a Thomas Lucas, at Mile End Green, Essex. Warrants were issued on 24 and 29 December 1597 for the arrest of Lucas, but he had fled to the continent and was later pardoned.

22 September 1598. A duel with swords took place between Ben Jonson, a playwright, and actor Gabriel Spenser. The reason for the duel is unknown, although it is believed to have been initiated by Spenser. During the fight, Spenser wounded Jonson in the arm, but Jonson struck back, stabbing Spenser in the right side, and killing him.

Jonson confessed to the killing, but escaped execution by pleading 'benefit of clergy', a provision which allowed clergymen to claim they were outside the jurisdiction of secular courts and to be tried in an ecclesiastical court under canon law. He was sentenced to be branded on the thumb.

8 November 1609. Sir George Wharton and Sir James Stuart fought a duel over a disagreement between them that broke out over a game of cards in Islington. Both men were killed.

December 1610. Sir Hatton Cheke and Thomas Dutton fought a duel in Calais, France. The duel resulted in the death of Cheke.

August 1613. A duel took place between Edward Bruce, the 2nd Lord of Kinloss, and Sir Edward Sackville, later to be 4th Earl of Dorset. They fought over the hand in marriage of Venetia Stanley. The duel took place in Bergen-op-Zoom, in Holland, to avoid the wrath of the king. Lord Bruce was killed, but the sting in the tail was that Venetia Stanley ended up marrying Sir Kenelm Digby, meaning Bruce's death was for nothing.

9 September 1613. A duel reportedly took place between Grey Brydges, 5th Baron Chandos, and Sir (Later to be Lord) James Hay, a favourite of King James I of England. If such an event did take place, it is clear that both men survived it, as Grey Brydges died on 10 August 1621, and James Hay passed away in March 1636.

13 May 1653. George Brydges, the 6th Baron Chandos, fought a duel against Colonel Henry Compton, who was killed during the fight. Chandos was found guilty of manslaughter and died whilst he was imprisoned.

16 January 1668. A duel took place at Barns Elm, Barnes, in London between George Villiers, 2nd Duke of Buckingham and Francis Talbot, 11th Earl of Shrewsbury. This resulted in the death of Shrewsbury, while George Villiers' second, Sir J. Jenkins, was killed by the earl's second. The duel took place because Villiers was having an affair with the Countess of Shrewsbury, the earl's wife.

9 April 1694. Edward Wilson challenged John Law to a duel over the affections of Elizabeth Villiers, who went on to become the Countess of Orkney. Wilson was killed in the duel. Law was arrested, tried and found guilty of murder and sentenced to death. His sentence was commuted to a fine on the grounds that the offence only amounted to manslaughter. Wilson's brother appealed and had Law imprisoned, but he managed to escape to the continent.

20 August 1698. Oliver Le Neve, a Norfolk country squire, fought a duel with Sir Henry Hobart on Cawston Heath, Norfolk, which resulted in Sir Henry's death. Le Neve escaped to Holland before he could be arrested. The background to the duel was over comments that had been made by both men about the other's reputation, and was the last recorded duel that took place in Norfolk. It was fought with swords, with Le Neve being wounded by a thrust to the arm, whilst Sir Henry was mortally wounded by a thrust to the stomach, and died the following day.

15 November 1712. What was known as the Hamilton-Mohun duel, took place in Hyde Park in London, and was between James Douglas, 4th Duke of Hamilton, and Charles Mohun, 4th Baron, which resulted in both of their deaths. Their seconds, George Macartney Esq, and Colonel John Hamilton, were charged and found guilty of manslaughter. The duel was the result of an argument between the two men as to who should succeed to the extensive estates of Fitton Gerard, 3rd Earl of Macclesfield, who had died without an heir.

July 1731. A duel which was about remarks each man had made about the other, took place between William Pulteney,

1st Earl of Bath and John Hervey, 2nd Baron Hervey. Both men survived.

17 December 1731. George Lockhart, a Scottish spy, writer and politician, was killed in a duel in Scotland. An article which appeared in the *Caledonian Mercury* dated Monday, 20 December 1731, states that he died at his home in Niddery's Wynd, but gave no account of how he died, although it was stated that he was from an ancient and honourable family. His father, Sir George Lockhart, was one of the most eminent lawyers of his time.

The following information appears on the website **www.historyofparliamentonline.org**

> Thereafter he lived quietly on his estates, until his abrupt and unexplained death by duelling on 17 December 1731. Neither the name of the challenger nor the location of the duel is known. The cause at issue is also obscure. The silence surrounding this affair nevertheless points towards a shameful family dispute.
>
> At the time of his death Lockhart is known to have been embroiled in two family quarrels. One dispute concerned the clandestine marriage of Lady Montgomerie, a daughter of the late Lord Eglington. As one of the Earl's executors, Lockhart had a particular interest in her future. He roundly condemned the use of an Episcopalian chaplain for the ceremony, which was contrary to law and might entangle the family in future difficulties. He also denounced the match as rash and unequal.

The bridegroom, Captain David Craig of Milnhall, may therefore have been the unknown duellist. An alternative explanation may be found in a longstanding rift between Lockhart and Lord Galloway. Some years previously, Galloway had made the scurrilous assertion that Lockhart's eldest son, George, had himself avoided a duel through indisposition with syphilis. Lockhart had rebuked Galloway, and is not known subsequently to have made his peace. The insult which led to the duel, whether involving Craig, Galloway or some other party, was probably made on 13 December 1731, at the funeral of Lady Panmure. The following day, Lockhart made an addendum to his will, a common act of preparation before duelling. His death passed without notice at the Stuart court. He had fallen from favour at the time of his retirement.

1736. A duel took place between Henry St Lawrence and Hamilton Gorges. It was Lawrence who had challenged Gorges, which cost the former his life. Gorges was tried for murder but was acquitted having claimed he had done so in self-defence.

12 March 1750. A duel took place between two Royal Naval officers, Captain Clarke and Captain Innis, which resulted in the latter's death. Clarke was tried and convicted of murder and sentenced to death, but received a Royal Pardon.

5 October 1762. John Wilkes and Samuel Martin fought a duel in Hyde Park. Martin, in his place in the House of Commons, had alluded to Wilkes as a 'stabber in the dark, a cowardly and malignant scoundrel'. Wilkes prided himself as much upon his gallantry as upon his wit and loyalty, and lost no time in calling Martin out. The challenge was given as soon as the House adjourned, and the parties repaired at once to a copse in Hyde Park with a brace of pistols. They fired four times, until Wilkes fell, wounded in the abdomen. His antagonist, relenting, hastened up and insisted on helping him off the ground, but Wilkes, with comparative courtesy, as strenuously urged Martin to hurry away, so as to escape arrest. It afterwards appeared that Martin had been practising in a shooting gallery for six months before making the obnoxious speech in the House; soon afterwards, instead of being arrested, he received a valuable appointment from the ministry.

26 January 1765. William Byron, 5th Baron Byron, fought a duel with William Charworth, his distant cousin, which saw the latter lose his life when Byron thrust a sword into his stomach. Byron was tried in the House of Lords, where he was acquitted of murder, but found guilty of manslaughter, for which he was fined. The quarrel which had led to the duel had been over the unimportant issue of which man had more game on his estate.

1772. Richard Brinsley Sheridan fought a duel with Captain Mathews, the result of a quarrel between the two men concerning Elizabeth Linley, to whom Sheridan was already secretly married. Initially they were to have the duel in Hyde Park, but it was too crowded. From there they went to the Castle Tavern in Covent Garden, where they fought with swords. Both men were cut, but neither was seriously wounded. Sheridan won the duel when Mathews pleaded for his life having lost his sword. They fought a second duel in July at Kingsdown near Bath to resolve the matter once and for all. Both men's swords broke, and Mathews stabbed Sheridan several times, seriously wounding him.

1783. Richard Martin, 'Humanity Dick', a nickname given to him by George IV, was said to have participated in over 100 duels, fought his cousin, James Jordan who had forced a duel. Martin shot him and he later died of his wounds.

1787. Sir John MacPherson and Major Browne fought a duel, when Browne, who had been a British resident at the court of Shah Alam II, took offence at his recall and challenged MacPherson, the former governor general of India, on the latter's return to Britain. A pistol ball passed through MacPherson's coat and another struck a pocketbook in his coat, but both men were uninjured.

26 May 1789. His Royal Highness Prince Frederick, Duke of York, fought a duel against Lieutenant Colonel Charles Lennox, after Lennox had called out the prince after accusing him of making 'certain expressions unworthy of a gentleman'. Lennox demanded a retraction of the allegations, which was refused. Lennox in turn demanded satisfaction, which resulted in the two men facing each other in a duel with pistols on Wimbledon Common. Lennox's shot 'grazed His Royal Highnesses' curl'. The prince then refused to take his shot stating that he had been called out to give satisfaction to Lennox and as satisfaction had been given, the matter was now closed.

12 July 1791. Mr John Graham, pleader of the Temple, challenged Richard Julius, attorney of Lincolns Inn, to a duel over a hypocrisy in affairs of gallantry. They met on Blackheath where Graham received a ball to his groin, which having severed his femoral artery, proved fatal. He died the following afternoon. The newspapers of the day were outraged.

Sometime in 1792. Lady Almeria Braddock and Mrs Elphinstone took part in what is historically referred to as the 'petticoat duel'. Lady Almeria Braddock felt insulted by Mrs Elphinstone and challenged her to a duel in London's Hyde Park, after their genteel conversation turned to the subject of Lady Almeria's true age.

The ladies first exchanged pistol shots in which Lady Almeria's hat was damaged. They then continued with swords until Mrs Elphinstone received a wound to her arm and agreed to write Lady Almeria an apology. An intriguing story, but one which the validity of is in question, as it appears there was no such person with the name of Lady Almeria Braddock, although there was a General Braddock who had a duel in Hyde Park with swords and pistols.

6 April 1803. A duel took place between Captain James Macnamara and Colonel Montgomery over a dispute between their dogs fighting in Hyde Park. Macnamara was walking his Newfoundland. There was an exchange of words between the two men, which led to a duel that evening at Chalk Farm. Both men were wounded, Montgomery fatally. Macnamara was tried for manslaughter at the Old Bailey and was acquitted after the court had heard from some thirteen witnesses, including knights of the realm, lords, viscounts and fellow naval officers.

7 March 1804. A duel took place between two friends, Captain Best and Thomas Pitt, 2nd Baron Camelford. The duel had come about because of an allegation that Best had made an uncomplimentary remark about Pitt to a lady he was seeing, and who had previously been Best's mistress. On hearing this, Pitt insulted Best and challenged him to a duel. The next morning they met at a café where Best asked Pitt to withdraw his remarks as they were friends, to which Pitt refused, not necessarily because he wanted to, but he knew that as Best was renowned for his skill with a pistol, he would lay himself open to allegations of cowardice if he now didn't go through with the duel. The two men faced each other on the morning of 7 March 1804, near to Holland House in Kensington. Pitt was hit in the chest with the shot passing right through him, severing his spine on exit. He died three days later. Pitt had made it clear in his will that in the case of their duel going against him, Best wasn't to be charged with his murder.

16 February 1821. A duel took place between John Scott, founder and editor of the *London Magazine*, and Jonathan Henry Christie. John Gibson Lockhart, a writer, had been abusing many of Scott's contributors in *Blackwood's Magazine* under the pseudonym of Z, as was common at the time. In May 1820, Scott began a series of counter-articles, which provoked Lockhart into calling him 'a liar and a scoundrel'. In February 1821, Lockhart's London agent, Jonathan Henry Christie, made a provocative statement, and Scott challenged him to a duel. They met on 16 February 1821, at a farm between Camden Town and Hampstead. Christie didn't fire in the first round, but there was a misunderstanding between the seconds, resulting in a second round. Scott was hit in the abdomen, and died eleven days later. Christie and his second were tried for wilful murder and acquitted.

August 1826. David Landale, a linen merchant from Kirkcaldy, took part in a duel with his bank manager, George Morgan, who had slandered his business reputation. This was the last duel ever fought in Scotland. George Morgan, a trained soldier, was shot through the chest and mortally wounded by Landale, who had never before held a pistol. Landale was tried for murder but found not guilty.

28 May 1841. A duel arose between Malachy Kelly, of Woodmount House, Tonalig, Co. Roscommon, and Owen Lynch, of Woodpark Lodge, Rathpeak, Co. Roscommon. It is understood that there was a dispute during a horse race meeting a few weeks earlier. The duel was held on Bellagill Bridge, Ballinasloe, over the River Suck on the Roscommon and Galway border on 28 May 1841. Malachy Kelly died of his wounds five days later on 3 June. This is the last known fatal duel to have taken place in Ireland.

Prior to writing this book, if somebody had told me that the duel of 1841 between Malachy Kelly and Owen Lynch had been the last ever such event on British soil, I would have no doubt accepted it without question as the date seemed to be in keeping with the final cessation of duelling. That is until I heard about another duel which took place more than 150 years later. The honour of having taken part in the last-known sword duel on British soil goes to Ben Salfield and an opponent named Edmund, who fought each other at Battle in East Sussex in August 1994. Below is a full account of this event, recounted by Ben in his own words

In August 1994 I had been on a trip to Battle in East Sussex for a firepower display by various re-enactment groups from across the UK. In 1994

I belonged to Sir Bevile Grenville's regiment in the Sealed Knot (the Civil War re-enactors) and at that time we probably had the best cannons in the UK.

When you 'live' the seventeenth century for days on end, especially as a lutenist specialising in repertoire from that era, you tend to begin *thinking* in a similar manner to those who had lived then – and perhaps, in an enclosed microcosm of society where the twentieth century did not exist, one might say we simply *continued*, rather than *re-enacted*, the seventeenth century for a short time.

So it came to pass that at the end of several days, a disparate bunch of re-enactors were drinking Spingo (a strong Cornish ale) around a campfire. One chap, a 6ft 7in tall, 25 stone-plus powerhouse, a bully called Edmund (who was also known by the nickname of 'The Beast') happened to make a derogatory comment about a young lady of my acquaintance at which I took umbrage. I demanded an apology, but he refused. I was still wearing my sword and had my hand on the hilt in anger, but one of my friends quickly placed his hand on my shoulder and said that this wasn't the way to go. For me it had now become a matter of honour, and so as any gentleman would do in such circumstances, I challenged him to a duel, which he readily accepted.

As he had been challenged, according to the rules of duelling, Edmund chose the weapons. I had hoped he might go for pistols so that we could both have fired in the air and gone home; unfortunately, he chose swords.

Seconds, a referee and witnesses were quickly found, and my second produced a pair of original seventeenth-century mortuary swords for the encounter, of which The Beast chose one. The duel was arranged for dawn the following morning, on a hillside close to the site of the Battle of Hastings.

That night I was urged to pull out of the encounter, as the odds on me winning were slim to say the least; but pride and honour won the day, and instead I wrote my will and waited in my tent for dawn, planning tactics with my second.

An hour before the allotted time, I rose and dressed in a Renaissance shirt and breeches, and walked slowly with my small band of supporters to the field. It had rained late in the night, leaving the air misty and cool, the scene was almost spooky as we awaited the arrival of my foe.

In due course, The Beast arrived with his small contingent, appearing out of the mist in a scene that could literally have been from 400 years earlier, and would have graced any Hollywood movie set.

At this point, everything seemed to happen incredibly quickly. We were reminded of the rules by the referee, the seconds checked the weapons, and a 4×4 was on stand-by, engine running, 30 feet away to transport any injured party to the nearest hospital. Before we commenced the duel, I offered Edmund one last opportunity to apologise for his insult, which he declined. Suddenly the duel was on, a battle that would actually last no more than four or five minutes but which felt so much longer.

Duelling is not like fencing, or at least it wasn't in my case. This huge man came in straight for the kill in an encounter that was supposed to be to 'first blood', that is, whomever spilled blood first was deemed to have lost. Edmund, though, seemed intent on causing me either serious injury or death. He launched a double-handed attack on me, trying to use his superior size and strength as he rained blows down on me from above in an apparent attempt to cleave my skull in two. All I could do was defend my head and retreat, scrambling backwards towards a small copse at the edge of the hillside field. Thinking quickly, I realised that his only weakness was that he was slower than me, and after defending seven or eight heavy blows, I could feel myself being worn down. I knew I had to pick one moment and make it count, and so that is exactly what I did. As he lifted his weapon one final time, I spotted his undefended left flank and slammed the blade of my sword into his rib cage as hard as I could. At that moment, the world appeared to move in slow motion. As he fell to the ground, the hilt of my sword smashed into his jaw. He hit the ground hard on his back and just lay there for a couple of seconds. A crimson patch appeared on his off-white shirt, and I knew I had won. In that split second I was momentarily overcome by a rush of adrenaline and I stood with my foot on his chest and roared triumphantly to the sky with my sword held to the heavens. I confess, it wouldn't have been difficult in that moment to have run him through as he lay on the ground.

Within seconds, the bystanders were with us, confiscating our swords and ripping open Edmund's shirt to check his wound. I put my hand out to him and tried to help him up, but he appeared to be more comfortable on the ground. He was conscious, though obviously in pain, and it was only then that he apologised for his prior affront. Honour had been duly satisfied.

The last time I ever saw Edmund he was being driven to A&E, although one of the people who went with him reported later that he had suffered two broken ribs, a laceration to the left hand side of his torso, a very sore jaw, and an even bigger bruised ego. I never saw any medical report so I cannot vouch for the veracity of these claims. I cannot imagine what he told A&E staff, but a re-enactment 'incident' wouldn't have been unknown.

Apparently, this was the last duel ever fought on UK soil, although twenty-four years later I did challenge someone else after they had published libellous claims about my character. On that occasion the person declined my challenge and apologised for any offence caused.

Duelling might sound like a barbaric pastime on the face of it, but I would argue the opposite. With rules in place and a controlled environment, it is perhaps more gentlemanly than the boxing ring. I personally consider it a brutal but fair way to decide a matter of honour.

Significant Duels in France

10 July 1547. A judicial duel took place between Guy Chabot de Jarnac and François de Vivonne de la Châtaigneraie on 10 July 1547. La Châtaigneraie was a favourite of the king and one of France's greatest swordsmen. During the fight, Jarnac fooled la Châtaigneraie with a feint and then caught him with a slash across his hamstrings. His dignity offended, la Châtaigneraie refused medical aid and died. This both ended the practice of trial by combat in France, and created the saying of, 'Le Coup de Jarnac', a strike that allowed amateurs to possibly defeat much better swordsmen.

12 May 1627. A duel took place at the Place Royale in Paris, France, between François de Montmorency-Bouteville and François d'Harcourt Beuvron without either being killed, but Montmorency-Bouteville's second, François de Rosmadec, Comte de Chappelles, duelled and killed Beuvron's second, the Marquis de Bussi d'Amboise. While Beuvron took refuge in England, Montmorency and Rosmadec, despite their nobility, were beheaded at the Place de Grève in Paris on 22 June 1627.

1641. A duel took place in France between Kenelm Digby and a French nobleman named Mont le Ros. Digby was attending a banquet when the Frenchman insulted Charles I of England. Digby challenged him to a duel. Digby later wrote that he had 'run his rapier into the French Lord's breast until it came out of his throat again', killing Mont le Ros instantly.

10 September 1718. An unusual duel took place, the likes of which I have previously never heard of. Two women duelling over a man. The Countess de Polignac and Marquise de Nesle fought a duel in the Bois de Boulogne, Paris in rivalry over the Duke of Richelieu. I was unable to establish the outcome of the duel, or even if the duke had shown a liking for either of the women. Whatever the outcome was, by 1729 he had begun an affair with Emilie du Chatelet.

As an addition to this but totally unconnected, another duel involving two women took place in France on 31 January 1772, when Mademoiselle de Guignes and Mademoiselle d'Aigullon fought a duel in Paris over a disagreement with each other. By all accounts it was a bloody affair. Neither of the women had seen fit to employ any seconds, which tends to suggest it was an either hastily arranged affair or a spontaneous one. The duel was fought with knives and resulted in both women being injured, Mademoiselle de Guignes in the arm and Mademoiselle d'Aiguillon in the neck. Both women survived the encounter.

Between 1794 and 1813. More than thirty duels were fought between the same two men: Pierre Dupont de l'Étang, who had been a general in the French army, the minister of war, as well as the minister of state, and François Fournier-Sarlovèze, who had also been a general in the French army. It had all begun with Fournier challenging Dupont after the latter had delivered a disagreeable message to his fellow officer. Dupont eventually overcame his opponent in a pistol duel, nineteen years later, and forced Fournier to promise never to bother him again.

20 September 1830. A story that made me smile, but one that also showed how classy the French people can be. The French writer Sainte-Beuve and one of the owners of *Le Globe,* Paul-François Dubois, fought a duel whilst it was raining heavily. Sainte-Beuve held his umbrella during the duel claiming that he didn't mind dying but that he wouldn't get wet.

23 February 1870. A duel took place between Édouard Manet and Louis Edmond Duranty. The latter, who was an art critic and a friend of Manet, had written only the briefest of commentary on two works of art that Manet had entered for exhibition. The frustrated Manet came across Duranty at the Café Guerbois, which during the 1800s was where artists, writers, and lovers of art would go to meet and discuss their passion for the arts. The café was situated on the Avenue de Clichy in Paris. Manet approached Duranty and slapped him round the face. Duranty demanded an apology, but Manet refused. This led to the pair fighting a duel with swords in the Forest of Saint-Germain-en-Laye, three days later on 23 February 1870. After Duranty received a wound above the right breast, the seconds, Émile Zola and Paul Alexis, who were both renowned French novelists, stepped in and declared that honour had been satisfied. The men remained friends despite the encounter.

13 July 1888. A duel took place between General Georges Boulanger and the prime minister of the French Republic, Charles Floquet. The duel took place after a heated argument over the revision of the French constitution. The general was wounded in the throat but survived, and Floquet's government fell in February the following year.

5 February 1897. A duel took place between French novelist, Marcel Proust and journalist, Jean Lorrain, after the latter had published an excoriating review of Proust's first book *Pleasures and Days*. He also hinted that Proust was having an affair with Madame Alphonse Daudet's son, Lucien. It isn't clear if it was what Lorrain had written about the novel, or his comments about Proust's alleged sexuality that enraged Proust. Proust and Lorrain exchanged shots at a distance of twenty-five paces. Proust fired first, hitting the ground by Lorrain's foot. Lorrain's shot missed, and their seconds both agreed that honour had been satisfied.

21 April 1967. The last official duel which took place in France happened on 21 April 1967 and was between Gaston Defferre and René Ribière, who were both delegates of the French National Assembly. During an argument in the assembly room, Defferre said to Ribière *'taisez-vous, abruti'*, which in English means, 'shut up, you idiot'. Ribière then challenged Defferre to a duel, which was won by the latter after just four minutes of sword fighting, during which time he had wounded Ribière twice.

Significant Duels in Germany

1704. The world-famous composer, George Frideric Handel, was nearly killed in a duel with Johann Mattheson. The two men were actually friends, but they got into a quarrel during a performance of Mattheson's opera, *Cleopatra*, which led to the two men duelling with swords. Handel was only saved by a large button on his jacket that deflected a blow from Mattheson's sword, which otherwise might have caused him a grave injury. The two men reconciled their differences and remained friends for the rest of their lives.

During the Second World War, Field Marshal Gunther von Kluge and General Heinz Guderian, were due to have a duel after a number of arguments took place between them during the preparations for the Battle of Kursk. It was von Kluge who challenged Guderian on 4 May 1943, after Guderian had refused to greet him at a conference attended by them both. Guderian accepted, but the duel never materialised as Hitler refused permission for it to go ahead.

Significant Duels in Italy

25 May 1552. Isabella de Carazzi and Diambra de Pottinella fought a duel as they were smitten by the same man, Fabio de Zeresola. The duel became famous and the object of a painting by Jusepe de Ribera, which he entitled, *Women Gladiators.* The two were Neapolitan noblewomen and were good friends until they fell out over de Zeresola, a man whom they were both seeing at the same time, a fact they only became aware of when they all attended the same wedding. Diambra challenged Isabella to a duel, which she accepted, and the women met about a week later. The duel took place on horseback, with both women equipped with a lance, sword and a mace. Everybody and anybody who was part of Naples' high society watched the events unfold. The initial contact between the two saw their lances glance off each other's shields. Diambra then struck Isabella with a mace; so powerful was the blow that it broke her shield in two, forcing her horse to stumble and Isabella to fall to the ground. Diambra then dismounted and demanded that her adversary surrender, and that Fabio was hers. In response, Isabella charged at her with her sword swinging and cutting the straps to Diambra's helmet, before conceding defeat.

27 October 1921. The subsequent Fascist leader of Italy, Benito Mussolini, fought a duel with swords with Francisco Ciccotti, who at the time was an editor of a Rome newspaper. The duel lasted an hour and a quarter and ended with Ciccotti unable to continue due to wounds received, and maybe mild exhaustion as well.

In Conclusion

Duelling has taken many forms over the years and involved thousands of individuals, so if theoretically each of them could be asked why they had actually taken part in a duel, and they answered honestly, most answers would more than likely include the word 'honour' at some point. But I would suggest that in most cases it had nothing to do with honour at all. Of course, these men had been wronged, or at least felt that they had been, but the reason for many of the duels was less to do with honour and more to do with either revenge, class or respect. It may even have been a desire not to miss out, as having taken part in a duel was almost like a badge of honour, or an exclusive old boys' club. A man who hadn't been involved in a duel might have been thought of as being 'not quite cut from the right stuff'.

As we know, duelling was the sole domain of nobility, aristocracy, gentlemen and the very rich and powerful of society, who saw themselves above common brawling. Two men of the lower classes who had a disagreement which each other, for whatever reason, might solve their differences by way of a brawl, trading blows until usually the stronger of the two would prevail and that would generally be the end of the matter. Gentlemen, however, didn't feel capable of conducting themselves in such a manner because they saw such behaviour as beneath them and demeaning. So for them, when they had a disagreement with another man, which was bound to happen at some stage of their lives, they needed a course of redress, and that was duelling. But even then there had to be a set of rules to give it a certain air of respectability.

If two men had a fight involving them rolling around on the floor, kicking and punching each other, then if one of the men died the one who survived would more than likely be found guilty of murder, and hanged, whereas a gentleman who had fought a duel with pistols where one man was killed, the survivor, even if arrested for murder, would, more often than not, claim self-defence and be found not guilty. This was even the case where a man shot first and missed, and then died when his opponent took his shot. How can that possibly be a case of self-defence?

Had there been no such thing as the aristocracy, nobility or gentlemen, the European version of duelling, which took place during the seventeenth, eighteenth and nineteenth centuries, may have never existed. That form of duelling was purely an attempt to prevent the upper echelons of society from resorting to fisticuffs, and thereby being no different to the common man. Such behaviour was just not acceptable to them, possibly because the manner in which they had been brought up in and the morals and values which they had instilled in them from a very young age.

About the Author

❖

Stephen is a happily retired police officer having served with Essex Police as a constable for thirty years between 1983 and 2013. He is married to Tanya, who is also his best friend.

Both his sons, Luke and Ross, were members of the armed forces, collectively serving five tours of Afghanistan between 2008 and 2013. Both were injured on their first tour. This led to his first book: *Two Sons in a Warzone – Afghanistan: The True Story of a Fathers Conflict*, which was published in October 2010. He also has a teenage daughter, Aimee.

Both his grandfathers served in and survived the First World War, one with the Royal Irish Rifles, the other in the Mercantile Navy, whilst his father was a member of the Royal Army Ordnance Corps during and after the Second World War.

Stephen collaborated with one of his writing partners, Ken Porter on a previous book published in August 2012, *German POW Camp 266 – Langdon Hills*. They have also collaborated on four books in the Towns & Cities in the Great War series by Pen and Sword. Stephen has also written other titles for the same series of books, and in February 2017 *The Surrender of Singapore – Three Years of Hell 1942–45*, was published. This was followed in March 2018 by *Against All Odds: Walter Tull the Black Lieutenant*. October 2018 saw the publication of *Animals in the Great War;* in January 2019, *A History of the Royal Hospital Chelsea 1682–2017 – The Warriors' Repose.* These last two books were written with his wife, Tanya.

Stephen has co-written three crime thrillers published between 2010 and 2012, and centre around a fictional detective named Terry Danvers.

When he is not writing, Stephen and Tanya enjoy the simplicity of going out for a morning coffee, or walking their German shepherd dogs early each day, whilst most sensible people are still fast asleep in their beds.

Index